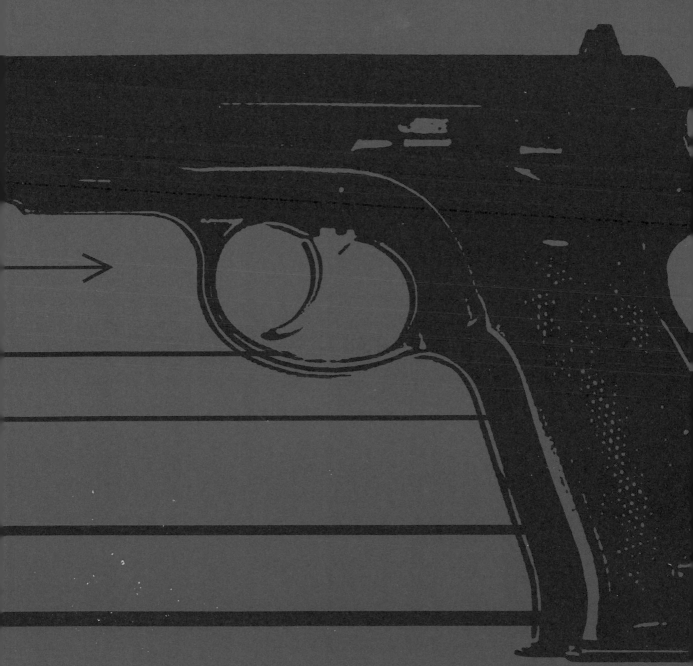

[spooks]
behind the scenes

First published in hardback in Great Britain in 2006
by Orion Books, an imprint of the Orion Publishing Group Ltd
Orion House, 5 Upper St Martin's Lane, London WC2H 9EA

The right of Kudos Film and Television Ltd to be identified as
the authors of this work has been asserted by them in accordance
with the Copyright, Designs and Patents Act 1988.

Copyright © Kudos Film and Television Ltd 2006

Written by Gaynor Aaltonen

10 9 8 7 6 5 4 3 2 1

A CIP catalogue record for this book is available
from the British Library.

ISBN-13: 978 0 75287 610 8
ISBN-10: 0 75287 610 4

Designed and typeset by Smith & Gilmour, London
Printed and bound in Great Britain by Bath Press

The Orion Publishing Group's policy is to use papers that are natural,
renewable and recyclable and made from wood grown in sustainable
forests. The logging and manufacturing processes are expected to
conform to the environmental regulations of the country of origin.

Every effort has been made to fulfil requirements with regard to
reproducing copyright material. The author and publisher will be
glad to rectify any omissions at the earliest opportunity.

www.orionbooks.co.uk

CONTENTS

MI5, NOT 9-5

> **For decades to come the spying world will continue to be the collective couch where the subconscious of each nation is confessed. John Le Carré**

Why has *Spooks* been such a roaring success? Why did more than nine million viewers turn on and tune in to that riveting first series? Why did millions more watch series four – champing at the remote control for series five?

Spying is a dark game, played out in cobwebs and lies. A furtive, hole-in-the-corner kind of business, where everything is anything but what it first seems, and where no one can be trusted, not even yourself. Acting – or pretending – is all; conflict is constant, and no one gets to know the truth till right at the end. Perfect for drama.

Add to this the fact that, post-9/11, spying is the new front line. When the planes hit the Twin Towers, the terrorists ripped up the rulebook. The world is now into 'asymmetric warfare', and all bets are off. The West's mighty ranks of aircraft, ships and tanks lie increasingly idle. This is war to the knife, but we're not going to win it by conventional means.

We need more spies than ever before: lots and lots of spooks in the enemy's camp. That was how the IRA eventually came to the peace table – and it's the only way moderates can beat the faith fascists. The double-agent has never been needed more – if only we could find the enemy camp to put them in, in the first place. Today, we hardly know who the enemy is.

Grounded in the bedrock of real life, *Spooks* gives us the fictional cutting edge in this blindfolded fight against terror. Not just the global, extremist religious kind, but also 'boutique terrorism' – the small special-interest group resorting to violence. Pro-life anti-abortionist Mary Kane and her husband 'killing in the name of saving life'; the nihilist, anti-human bombers 'Shining Dawn', killing for what they believe is the greater good; gun-runners branching out into supplying Al-Qaeda; and let's not forget the extreme right-wing. Even the big corporations are at it in *Spooks*, prepared to take out the opposition with a handy missile.

Inside the big thematic tent of the front-line war to defend the realm, the double-agent fuels the show. Like the real MI5, our fictional *Spooks* have to take on and defeat these myriad threats, and the way they do it best is by wearing the mask. Tom and Helen (*right*), posing as 'IT trainers', using charm to scotch vicious right-wing racist George Osborne. Getting only too close, in Helen's case. That's the risk you take when you put on the spook's motley. Zoe too plays the double role, till eventually she is in such danger that she loses her cool – and her job.

The mask also drives – and destroys – our spooks' personal lives. They have problems we all share. Juggling work and relationships; disagreeing with your boss; avoiding tiresome old school friends you meet in the street. But – and this is where the show hits hard – being a spook means all of these problems are hugely magnified. This is the reality of living the lie. Being false to your loved ones, day in and day out. Waking up with the mask, and going to bed with it. Only getting to take it off at work – which is to say, when you are with all the other liars. As world-weary Harry says: 'In this job, we have no friends.' How does that feel? How does it make you feel about yourself? Tom tells us.

Every week, the country's values and our way of life get tested to destruction. But then thanks to the skill, courage, cunning and bold-faced deceit of our spooks, that same beleaguered society survives. Hard fact underpins and enhances the high-octane, full-spectrum thriller storylines *Spooks* does so well. The combination is hard to resist. The series has also been a monster hit in the USA, where it is re-named *MI5*, and has been screened across the world, from Russia [with love, obviously] to – would you believe it – Iran.

This is rich story ground – and we all know it. That's why we watch ... Is this eerily prescient show preparing us for a terrifying real-life future?

LICENCE
TO THRILL

THE BIRTH OF A SERIES...

A new millennium, a new world order. Back in the ice-encrusted days of the Cold War spying was a major international industry, and everybody knew the rules of the game. But come the year 2000, spies and their masters were feeling the chill. With the Berlin Wall down, and the Northern Ireland conflict coming to an end, the security services seemed about as relevant as the dinosaur. The horrific events of 11 September 2001 were yet to unfold, but for those who were reading the runes, this was the calm before a firestorm.

'This was at a time when the intelligence services were suddenly having to fight to maintain budgets and resources,' says Stephen Garrett (*right*) – the man who first had the idea of creating a series called *Spooks* – 'yet there we were, developing our idea for a series ...'

The fertile minds of scriptwriters on both sides of the Atlantic were working in tandem. Garrett's production company, Kudos, got word there was also a series in development in the States about the CIA. The BBC was developing a similar idea called *5* in direct competition with *Spooks*. Fox, meanwhile, was making the radical *24*, starring Keifer Sutherland. What did the 'creatives' know that the rest of the world didn't? 'Extraordinarily, *24* had a plane blowing up in the very first episode,' says Garrett. [It had to be pulled.]

'We were green-lit just a month before 9/11,' says executive producer Simon Crawford Collins. 'Everyone was devastated, of course, on the day it happened. We were all shocked, like the whole country. We went in to have a crisis meeting with the BBC, to see if we should carry on. The view came back that what we were doing was really relevant. This was what drama is all about – facing up to crises. And this challenge to society was the biggest of our times.'

So along came Tom, Danny and Zoe – modern gladiators, stepping out into the arena to fight with courage, skill and scruple for their country's cause. Right?

Wrong. After Le Carré and Graham Greene, we all know that spies can't afford the luxury of the bright, shining sword of truth. Their world is one of danger, distrust and dystopia. Uncertainty rules. And as the clock ticks and the world turns, the spooks become more knowing, more ruthless, and more cynical: their decisions ever more difficult.

In the first series, lofty Tessa Phillips has set herself up with a nice little earner in phantom informants. Who'd have thought it? Well, just about anyone who watches the show. Or knows any real spies. But a few years down the track, and Tessa's dishonesty seems almost innocent.

That was then. This – post-Abu Ghraib, post-dodgy dossiers, and after the public humiliation of at least two Home Secretaries in a row – is the ever more murky here and now.

In series one, it takes trusty novice Danny Hunter no time to bump his credit rating up when he thinks no one's looking. [Someone's always looking, Danny...] By the time Adam comes to run the team, the rules of the game are getting harder even than those that combined to destroy Tom. By series three, our heroes are using torture.

Britain's real-life plans for a National Identity Register seem to threaten not just our privacy, but our liberty. If the government merges all its Civil Service databases into one, someone with the right 'access' could surf between health and education records to the tax and vehicle registration databases at will. Roll on series five...

FIRST STEPS TO A SERIES

Stephen Garrett first had the idea for *Spooks* when he was browsing in a bookshop. Astonished at the sheer number of books written about espionage and the lives of spies, he started thinking. Then, again by chance, he met writer David Wolstencroft, whom he had already worked with on the successful series *Psychos*. It turned out David was researching spying, too.

'You know that phrase, "Failure is an orphan, but success has many parents..." Well, that couldn't be truer in television, and it couldn't be truer of *Spooks*,' Garrett says. 'It's the only really creative idea I've ever had, so I want to hang on to the credit! But on something like this, every one of the talented people along the way – writers, directors, actors – create it, too.

'Originally, I was more interested in the idea of their private lives. Sort of *This Life* meets *Spooks*. I'd been thinking: what happens if you go to a party, and you meet someone? What if you'd like to try and pick someone up? It intrigued me: what could you do? These are people who effectively have to lie all the time in their private lives, as well as spending their whole working life as a lie – and that fascinated me.'

The BBC was already vaguely interested in Kudos doing something along the lines of a precinct-based drama. But it wasn't as simple as all that. 'The two classic "precincts", where you have life and death situations coming through your doors 24/7, are police headquarters, or hospitals,' Garrett says. 'But they said we couldn't do police, and we couldn't do hospitals – there were so many of those already.'

At this time, a new head of drama commissioning, Gareth Neame, arrived at the BBC and Jane Featherstone joined Kudos as the new head of drama. Both of them had the desire to make *Spooks* a bigger and more real life thriller behind the intelligence of the contemporary world.

And then 9/11 happened. David explains: 'MI5 were already juggling. And then someone threw a bowling ball at them.'

The world changed with the team already well into writing series one. 'We clearly had a responsibility to integrate this new dimension of global life into the show,' says Wolstencroft. 'So we went back and contextualised the entire series with this in mind. Actually, in many ways the scenario was pretty close to the reality: MI5 was in existence, working away on the kinds of things we were already writing about.'

As Harry Pearce says in the very first lines of the opening episode:

> **Global terrorism, Islamic extremists, all phone-tap resources plus Echelon pointed at the Middle East, and now the old enemy looks like it's rearing its ugly head...and it's such a beautiful morning...**

'...That speech got added on at the end.'

The creative team had done their research; they knew their characters. So they hit the ground running.

SO ARE THERE ANY RULES?

'One of the reasons *Spooks* works so well is that people know, when someone's in danger, they really might die,' says Garrett. 'Because it does kill its loved ones.'

'We wanted to create a fast-paced show,' says Crawford Collins. 'So fast that you had to keep your wits about you. The more research we did, the more we realised there is a huge story here. The whole job of a spy involves sensitive political and moral issues. And when it comes to the characters themselves, what drives people to get involved in such a murky and dangerous world is a story in itself.'

Getting close to the truth mattered. 'One thing we learned by talking to ex-security personnel was the incredible length of time they have to spend on projects. They spend months and months just researching – each part of an operation could build up over a period of years. We've had to massively compress the time frame. So we know it isn't fully real – but we did do our homework.

'We learned about an embassy based in a Georgian terrace, for instance. When MI5 discovered that a house six doors away was for sale, they drilled through the attic beams with a silent drill – using technology that initially came from the oil industry. They had to get through the joists of six houses to achieve the target. The drilling operation alone took them six months – a month per house.

'For guidance we had two agents: one from MI5 and one who was ex-CIA. We got a lot of technical advice of course, but some of the best bits were the fascinating anecdotes, and practical suggestions about the security services' ways of doing things.

'Peter Salter [played by Anthony Head], for instance. He's a highly trained agent who knows he's being watched. How would someone like him shake the surveillance off? The scriptwriter, Howard Brenton, called our contact. Simple! Just ring up the police and complain: there's a couple "doing it" [Zoe and Danny – no, they weren't] in this car in a residential street, and there might be children about...'

THAT WAS THEN – THIS IS NOW

In the war on terror, intelligence is the most vital currency of all. But intelligence, like 'a little learning', can be a dangerous thing. 'Intelligence is very rarely 100 per cent,' says Sir John Walker, a former chief of defence intelligence. 'Very rarely do you get a black and white picture. You're normally playing pretty heavily in the greys...'

March 2003: Britain and the USA declare war on Iraq. The previous September, the Joint Intelligence Committee had produced a report on Saddam Hussein's 'weapons of mass destruction'. The so-called 'dodgy' dossier had so many of the 'ifs and buts' or 'greys' removed; it was a propaganda tool instead of a reasoned report. This was an alarming first for the intelligence services.

'Iraq was an aberration,' Sir John said on BBC radio. 'It was the first time, as far as I know, that intelligence has been bent or politicised to make a point.'

Chemical bombs, home-made in Walthamstow, 7/7, Abu Hamza...alarming headlines like the *Telegraph*'s of June 2006: 'MI5 fears silent army of 1,200 biding its time in the suburbs.' You could argue that it was abuse of intelligence by the UK government that has led Britain into danger. Which just goes to show how dangerous 'intelligence' is...

WHAT OF THE FUTURE?

What will happen next? Can Harry and Adam keep their score sheet clean under the relentless pressure? You can always trust David Wolstencroft to take a question seriously. 'Everybody gets religion,' he says. 'They all become Quakers, and go and live in Norwich...

'All I can say is that subconsciously we seem to have followed the contours of society's response to 9/11. The first series was about "defending the realm", in the context of a catastrophe that everybody was still absorbing. Series two explored a landscape of counter-terrorism – okay, now we've got to go and get the bad guys. The third stepped back a pace: if our society is going to have to live with this threat, then how does it affect our own lives? We're writing a series about espionage in the UK, but in a sense, espionage is a way of telling you about the UK.'

Crawford Collins agrees: 'The big thing with series three was trusting the state, and to what extent that was a good or a bad thing. Although MI5 and MI6 are technically independent of the government of the day, government was getting very interested in the way the intelligence services worked. With the Iraq war, the Hutton enquiry and everything that was happening at the BBC, that turned out to be a very big issue.

'In series four, civil liberties came to the fore: how far should the intelligence services really go to protect people?'

And series five? 'I think we're all wondering to what extent democratic government as we've known it can continue to function in the face of these huge problems – terrorism, fuel crises, immigration, the environmental issues. Is the nice, cosy method of government that's worked so well over so many hundreds of years – is that going to continue?'

HANSARD
House of Commons Standing Committee 2 Dec 2004
Subject: GPS systems and the Galileo Project. A rival to the existing Global Positioning System (GPS, *right*), run by the United States. Like the Russian Glonass system, GPS is a military-run network and can be downgraded or taken offline if an enemy attempts to use the data to launch guided missiles, for example. By contrast, Galileo will be a civilian-run operation.

BARBARA FOLLETT Does my Hon. Friend get a chance to watch television? If so, he will see from shows like *Spooks* or *24* the applications the technology has. The Galileo technology has huge applications for crime prevention and detection. It is used an enormous amount to track lost children or adults.
MR JAMIESON I have seen the trailers for *Spooks* and that has been sufficient for me to decide not to watch it. I am more of a *Heartbeat* type.
THE CHAIRMAN You sad person.

THE LIFE OF A SPY

' You know, Rick, I have many a friend
in Casablanca, but somehow, just
because you despise me, you are the
only one I trust. **Peter Lorre as
Guillermo Ugarte in Casablanca** ,

YOUR DINNER
IS IN THE CAT . . .

The world's second-oldest profession, spying is more than a bit like the most ancient. But in spying – or at least in *Spooks* – you do get to save the state on a weekly basis. Then there's your colleagues, who are hunky, handsome and glamorous – except possibly for Malcolm, who has finely honed joke-telling skills; and Colin, who is good with bits of wire and can shoot straight.

In reality, as in *Spooks*, the life of an operational spy – at home or abroad – is generally dangerous, grubby and destructive of the self. Spies – or rather field officers and their agents – have to live the lie. This is tricky. None of us, deep down, is quite what we present to the world, even to our nearest and dearest. But with spies it's official – there is no escape from the corridors of deception, and the penalty for letting slip the mask can be death – or worse. Whom can you trust, outside the blast-proof walls?

Once you have been trained to do it, lying is very difficult to give up – even worse than smoking. Trained to lie themselves, spies tend to suspect everyone else has got the habit, including their loved ones. [They are lying sometimes too, of course – but not always.]

'Stress is endemic in intelligence work,' said former MI5 officer Miranda Ingram after a trial in the 1980s. 'You are trained to be suspicious, to assume the worst motive in the simplest of actions. Those attitudes can be very difficult to shake off at the end of the day, and you may find yourself doubting the honesty of a friend who tells you he is going out to buy a pint of milk, particularly as you are expected to lie to this same friend about the nature of your work.'

This constant pressure to remember to forget who you really are; the need to live inside a secret skin, is bound to take its toll on relationships that matter; which as we all know only work if they are based in truth. Countless spies describe the breakdown of their relationships under this weight. Double-agent George Blake, who escaped from Wormwood Scrubs and a forty-two-year sentence in 1966, vividly describes his horror when his wife first became pregnant. In his dangerous position, he should never have had children at all. But he couldn't explain this to his wife without telling her the truth:

TOM I had the wrong wallet with me tonight. I almost paid for dinner as Tom Quinn. Which seeing as Ellie thinks she's going out with Matthew Archer might have seemed a little odd to her. (*beat*) I can't do this for much longer.
HARRY You've not had a problem before.
TOM Well I've not felt like this about anyone before.
HARRY If you'd told us the truth in the first place, of course ... the vetting would be over by now.
TOM I just wanted to keep things simple.
HARRY Always a mistake. In my experience.

LYING FOR A LIVING

In *Spooks*, Tom, Zoe and Christine all come a cropper when one or more of the lies they have to inhabit catches up with them. It's only in Tessa's case that the deception – and her fall – is entirely of her own making. For everyone else, it is the job and the relentless pressure.

Fear, loneliness, paranoia, deception and mistrust: all of this is a recipe for serial relationship disaster. The failure to tell the new love of his life, Ellie, who and what he is sees Tom Quinn start the series – and his love life – on entirely the wrong foot. The lie makes him vulnerable; makes Ellie suspicious; leads to conflict and hard words; mistrust, mistake and the slow-mo, horribly fascinating train crash that is the end of the affair.

In the crushing, almost epic destruction of Tom, Herman and Carmen Joyce make up a lie-web so colossal and complete that even Tom's own team believe it. He ends up on the run, accused of murder and sacked: small reward for all his sterling effort and loyalty.

Zoe lies on oath, in court (*left, top*), about the true nature of her mission to penetrate the Turkish mafia – but the perjury doesn't save her. The greater truth – that she made a mistake, strayed beyond her brief, and is trying to hide that – brings her crashing to earth. The truth will out. Eventually.

Human beings aren't made to keep up this level of deception long-term: we like to be ourselves, now and again. Which is one of the ways in which *Spooks* scores: no one is James Bond, or superhuman; these are real people, who happen to have an extreme job. But if you are going to live the lie, then you have to be the best at it, like legendary former agent Angela Wells [episode 4.10]. Here endeth the first lesson of *Spooks* – one of many we learn from the series.

REAL LIFE, REAL PRESSURES

Spying, like police work, is time-hungry and unpredictable. It's pretty hard to explain, as Tom discovers to his cost, exactly why you missed your own birthday party and came by a nasty flesh wound when you are only supposed to be fixing computers. Absence from home – often with little or no warning – for days or weeks at a time is not the best way of keeping your friends, partners and families happy.

Former government intelligence analyst Lieutenant-Colonel Crispin Black agrees: 'Surveillance in particular is a hard work/no glamour business – long hours of sour coffee and takeaways in freezing and dingy streets. Neither Irish nor Islamist terrorists tend to hang out in the tonier parts of town.'

The series' mystery MI5 and CIA advisers, says David Wolstencroft, were very, very clear. We viewers might have been brought up on *NYPD Blue* and *Cracker*, where the good guys assemble evidence, and then get the bad guys at the end. But in reality, getting the enemy behind bars can be fiendishly difficult.

'It's not always about "bringing them to justice",' says Wolstencroft. 'Sometimes it's about using the bad guys to win in another, more complex game with higher stakes. Sometimes it's just about stuffing them, by using one lot against the other. Once you realise that, everything is possible, and the sneakier or the cleverer the better.'

Many real-life accounts aired by ex-MI5 officers describe it as a sclerotic bureaucracy, whose middle management is so risk-averse that every decision has to be referred up and down a coagulated hierarchy. Until, as often as not, it comes back in its original state. By which time, the terrorists may have exploded a half-ton of fertiliser bomb that could have been prevented given fast, decisive action.

If the stress does make you snap, the Security Service has not, historically, been good at providing help. Despite his habitual lunchtime sessions in the pub, senior managers failed to notice that 1980s MI5 officer Michael Bettaney had a drink problem, and ignored other warning signs of breakdown. When he started chucking secret files over the walls of the Soviet Embassy, Bettaney finally got everyone's attention – if not quite the kind he needed. Arrested and tried in 1984, Bettaney got twenty-four years in prison. The subsequent Security Commission report slated MI5's management of its 'human resources'.

'I wanted you to work it out, Danny, get it through your system...This thing you have with money. Particularly money that you don't have. We all have our little quirks. And ingenious theft – like breaking into computers to set your own credit rating - isn't such a sin in our trade. It's an impulse that, creatively channelled, could be used to brilliant effect. Sadly in your case it has not - yet. **Harry Pearce** ,

Another drawback to real spying is the fact that you tend not to get paid all that well, unless you wriggle to the top of the slippery pole, when private health insurance, a much better pension and an office with a view of the river cut in. Is this why so many real spies turn to the bad?

In real-world espionage, the worst case of a double-agent's duplicity – in terms of its cost in human suffering – is probably CIA turncoat Aldrich Ames (*left*). Ames's prime motivator was indeed money. More precisely, his second wife Rosario's demands for it. To fuel an extravagant lifestyle he could not afford on his official salary, Ames betrayed most of the CIA's agents inside the Soviet Bloc. For the sake of his and Rosario's $540,000 home, unworn designer suits, and a few hundred pairs of shoes, Ames had his countrymen and colleagues rounded up by the KGB, interrogated, and in many cases tortured and killed.

And there's the rub: you can be as good as you like at the spying game, but if a fellow spook has gone over to the other side, you can and will get fried. Ames joked at his trial that there was no one left to trade for him – he'd already shopped them all. Dead funny.

WARNING: DANGEROUS ROAD AHEAD

If you are up at the sharp end – inside the cell with the enemy – a false word or look can catch you a bullet in the back of the neck. Or get your feet beaten to a pulp, as Johnny, Tom's too young, too inexperienced informer inside the Birmingham mosque, discovers to his terrible cost [episode 2.2]. Your 'secret skin' has to be spotless – and watertight. Spying can ruin your life expectancy. In *Spooks*, leaving aside a rash of mere flesh wounds, the bullet takes Herman and Carmen Joyce [ex-spies who can't give up the adrenalin-rush of the job], Danny Hunter, Fiona Carter, and a host of supporting characters out of the spying game for good. Adam Carter's [literally] tortured past was inspired by the true story of CIA station chief William Buckley, who was horribly murdered in the Lebanon. Episodes 4.1 and 4.2 are carnage city, with a near-*Dirty Harry* body count.

But some people come to love that danger. Robert Philip Hanssen (*right*) was betrayed by a Russian double-agent some years after Ames. Before he joined the FBI, Hanssen had been one of Chicago's finest – a cop, a devoted father and a loving husband, who attended Catholic mass with exemplary regularity. 'He was brilliant and he looked like an altar boy,' recalled a contemporary. Undetected for nearly twice as long as Ames, this cherubic figure betrayed field agents, FBI techniques and 6,000 pages of US secrets. Hanssen's is an interesting case, because unlike Ames he lived a pretty modest lifestyle.

But Hanssen plunged into a risky double life. In 1990 he met stripper Priscilla Sue Galey. Within days he was giving her stacks of the KGB's $100 bills. She used the first $2,000 to get her teeth fixed.

While his wife Bonnie still drove a beaten-up minivan, Hanssen bought his stripper friend a sleek, silver Mercedes. Next came an American Express card. For Christmas, he gave her a diamond and sapphire gold necklace. 'She would ask him about where he got all that money,' her mother, Linda Harris, told the press. 'He would always laugh and say: "I could tell you, but then I would have to kill you."'

Galey always claimed that Hanssen never tried to seduce her. Far from that, he tried to get her to go to church. When he took her on a two-week trip to Hong Kong he insisted on separate flights and rooms. But one night in a hotel bar, Galey did manage to persuade him to dance. The music? 'As Time Goes By', from the ultimate espionage film, *Casablanca*. Had he become addicted to risk? It happens.

THRILL SEEKERS

When Hanssen realised he was rumbled he wrote his controllers a note straight out of John Le Carré:

Dear Friends:
I thank you for your assistance these many years. It seems, however, that my greatest utility to you has come to an end, and it is time to seclude myself from active service. I have been promoted to a higher do-nothing Senior Executive job outside of regular access to information within the counterintelligence program. I am being isolated. Further, I believe I have detected repeated bursting radio signal emanations from my vehicle. Amusing the games children play.

He was right about his car. A surveillance team had already watched him drive by the entrance to the park four times, waiting for the white strip of tape that would signal his Russian handlers were ready to receive his package. Five days before he was due to 'retire', Hanssen was caught. $50,000 in non-sequential $100 bills had been waiting for him in Foxstone Park, less than a mile from his home.

STARING INTO DANGER

Exotic dancer Mata Hari, the most renowned female spy in history, was executed by a French firing squad in 1917. As the men prepared to shoot, she blew them a farewell kiss. Not everyone can show such bravado. Fair Zoe, whose looks frequently land her some of the most difficult jobs as a deep cover 'swallow', gets her own peep over the edge of the abyss in episode 3.6. She promptly falls into it out of pure fear, ordering would-be lover Sevilin Ozal to kill terrifying mafia boss Emré Celenk. Will it all end in wedding bells, an inglenook and Zoe at the stove with a cuddle of babies round her feet? Well, no.

Tessa's reaction to the pressures of espionage is to bite the hand that feeds her. But unlike Zoe, she enjoys it. This is the world of Kim Philby and Aldrich Ames – the white-knuckle ride that is cheating in plain sight: lying, scheming and betraying right under the noses of your highly trained spy colleagues. A study from the USA's Center for Counterintelligence and Security suggests that thrill-seeking is a major factor in the lives of most traitors.

Which is why your fellow spies keep looking over your shoulder. Not just to check that you are doing your job, but to make sure you haven't turned – or been turned – to the dark side for money, sex, or simply for the thrill of it.

But there is one thing that beats even the roller-coaster life of risks…

THE SPY WHO LOVED ME

Fiona Carter always gives the impression she relishes danger. Faced with a threat to Adam, she gambles her own life to face down her vicious former husband. A very bad bet: Fiona wins the battle, and loses her life.

But the majority of women who turn to real-world spying do it not for the kicks, but for the big 'L' – love. Sent to work as secretary of the CIA chief in Ghana, a shy, naïve clerk named Sharon Scranage fell in love with a cousin of Ghana's President, Flight Lieut. Jerry Rawlings. Why was big fish Michael Soussoudis, a handsome and influential 'businessman', interested in a humble clerk? The thirty-nine-year-old Soussoudis was, of course, an undercover intelligence agent. The 'honeytrap' victim gave him an entire database disclosing the identities of all the CIA's agents in the country. She also passed her lover CIA cables, including one giving details of a planned coup.

Arrested in 1985 when she failed a routine CIA staff polygraph test, Scranage ended up in a women's penitentiary...Sic transit spy.

THE BODY POLITIC?

' Men's minds, of course, are shaped by their environment and we spies, although we have our professional mystique, do perhaps live closer to the realities and hard facts of international relations than other practitioners of government. We are relatively free of the problems of status, of precedence, and evasion of personal responsibility which create the official cast of mind. We do not have to develop, like the Parliamentarians conditioned by a lifetime, the ability to produce the ready phrase, the smart reply and the flashing smile. And so it is not surprising these days that the spy finds himself the main guardian of intellectual integrity. [quoted in George Blake's autobiography *No Other Choice*] '

Blake claims this was an internal circular issued by SIS vice-chief George Young. The words would hardly be out of place in Harry Pearce's mouth. Harry regularly has a conscience attack:

HARRY You'll call off the dogs. It ends here, now. All of it. Unless you want this to hit the presses.
JULIET You wouldn't do that.
HARRY Try me.

The series' aim is to examine the dark and dubious ways that the 'environment' George Blake once knew has changed. Politicians, post-Iraq war, post 'dodgy-dossier', are attempting to manipulate the system:

HICKS The way our political system's degenerated ... The lies, the spin ... Iraq, the whole politics of fear thing – dirty bombs and the rest of the fantasies the government keeps coming up with to justify their existence and make them look like self-righteous heroes.
(*beat*) He called it—
HARRY Velvet fascism. I know.

Political interference with the 'intellectual integrity' of the spy is a major theme of *Spooks*.

A NEW ERA

MI5 has stopped at least an alleged four major terrorist attacks in London recently, including a multiple attack on trans-Atlantic airliners, and there are strong signs that it is a reformed organisation. The 'Forest Gate' fiasco of 2006, a dramatic 200-strong police raid with little to substantiate it, may just have been an unfortunate glitch.

It would be nice to believe that *Spooks*, glamorous, exciting and packed to the gills with chisel-featured decision-makers of both sexes, is dragging MI5 into an era of positive change. When it started, the series certainly gave recruitment a major shot in the arm, roughly doubling applications overnight – until, that is, our fictional *Spooks* began to break down, lose out in love, get wounded and die.

Through its four series, *Spooks* has trained a hard eye on the morals of both state and Security Service, questioning and probing the major issues of our time. They range from immigration to racism; 'extraordinary rendition' to the environment; the UK's dependent relationship with the United States; the insidious nature of 'spin'; major social projects like the National Health Service; the growth of crackpot ideologies and religious extremism.

As Harry makes clear, when Zoe prepares for a life in prison following her one big mistake, being part of MI5 means total commitment. And total self-sacrifice:

HARRY It's very complex. Much more is at stake here.
ZOE Than my liberty and my career?
HARRY Yes.

Still think you fancy the life of a spy? Good luck.

MI5/SIS
HISTORY

SECRETS MIGHTIER THAN THE SWORD

People talk about 'The Fog of War' but the 'fog index' around the secret world of British intelligence could hardly be murkier. The Security Service has many identities, just like its officers and agents. Also known as 'Box' and 'The Office', MI5 is an organisation obsessive in its secrecy and ruthless in its deceit. Themes that are the life-blood of *Spooks* ...

'He who knows his adversary as well as he knows himself will never suffer defeat. Sun Tzu – *The Art of War*, 6th century'

WHAT'S IN A NAME?

'M.I.' and the shorthand terms MI5 and MI6 stands for 'Military Intelligence'. In 1916 the Secret Service Bureau became part of a larger directorate. Military Intelligence 1 was responsible for code-breaking; '2' was for Russia and Scandinavia, and '3' for the rest of Eastern Europe. MI4 was an aerial reconnaissance department. The SSB's 'home' and 'foreign' sections became MI5 and MI6 respectively. Lots of these functions were later absorbed into the War Office or into GCHQ, and the titles are now completely defunct. The two organisations have not, however, managed to shake off the vestigial names.

The enigmatic 'M' in Ian Fleming's James Bond books has his origins with the head of the Secret Service Bureau's foreign section, 'C'. The original 'C', Mansfield—Cumming, signed himself simply 'C' at the end of a document in green ink, and his MI6 successors have carried on the tradition. When Fleming was writing in the 1950s, the 'C' of the time would have been first Major—General John Sinclair (fired within a mere three years) and then the handsome but unassuming Dick White. The Russian spy Kim Philby scathingly said of White: 'His most obvious fault was to agree with the last person he spoke to.' We can safely assume that Fleming's daunting and masterful 'M' was not precisely modelled on either character.

It is also possible that using the letter 'M' was Fleming's way of paying homage to William Melville, spy extraordinaire. Melville was the press's favourite, an Edwardian—era hero who as a top policeman had been involved in many juicy scandals and arrests, and someone who knew how to play dirty. When he became part of the Secret Service Bureau under Vernon Kell, Melville put a professional thief on the staff, to teach his new recruits to do their jobs.

Your Country Needs You...

A century ago, with the world on the edge of total war, two British
officers were plucked from obscurity and told to create a Secret Service
Bureau. It was to be the world's first official intelligence service.

A wave of anti-German hysteria was hitting Britain. It was not
unfounded. Expansionist Germany was, in fact, sending spies across the
Channel to gather intelligence on the Royal Navy's ships and installations.

The new secret service, founded in 1909, was to have an army branch
and a naval one [the Royal Air Force only came into being in 1918].
Ascetic and manipulative, the brilliant British Army Captain Vernon Kell
spoke German, Polish, Italian, French and some Russian – but was really
known as a Chinese specialist. In the series, Zoe, of course, is a Serbo-
Croat and German linguist, Ruth speaks demotic French and reasonable
Arabic, while Adam and Fiona are both fluent Arabic speakers.

Royal Navy Commander Mansfield Cumming was a bit of a contrast to
Kell. Retired from active service because of poor health, Cumming – or 'C' –
had a reputation for dangerous driving, and had to have his leg amputated
after a road accident in France that killed his son. He was working in naval
research when he was first approached to head up the foreign section of
the new bureau. 'C' took responsibility for overseas operations, Kell for the
fight against espionage at home. Until quite recently, MI5's head of
counter-espionage was still called 'K' after Kell. To this day, the chief of
MI6 is still known as 'C'.

Another mysterious figure hangs over this story – the 'M' of James Bond
fame. Former Metropolitan Police Superintendent William Melville (*right*)
was Britain's first real intelligence officer in the mould of a Tom Quinn or
an Adam Carter. A flamboyant, Scarlet Pimpernel character, Melville had

the knack of being everywhere and seeing everything. With the First World War looming Germany was building a fleet of thirty-six dreadnoughts, and Melville was asked to hunt down a nest of suspected German spies intent on stealing information about British shipping lanes, ship movements and naval technology. So Melville got creative. As he went around the country he began writing the rules of the spying trade: recruiting landladies, adopting cover identities and befriending the suspects.

Meanwhile, Kell had had an immense stroke of luck. One of his officers had overheard a conversation on a train – a lucky chance that would eventually land thirty-five enemy agents in jail. Stanley Clarke sat next to two Germans discussing an incomprehensible letter one of them had received. It asked about British preparations for war. When Clarke approached them, they gladly handed the letter over: it was from a 'Mrs Reimers'.

The 'lady' in question turned out to be Gustav Steinhauer, a senior member of German Intelligence. It took three years of hard work, learning how to decipher invisible inks on innocent-looking documents, and tracking down the members of what was obviously a major spy ring in the making. But eventually, Kell cracked it, along with the postmaster general of the ring, Karl Gustav Ernst.

By 1914, when John Buchan's spy story *The Thirty-nine Steps* was serialised, the country was at a fever pitch of excitement and fear. With rumours of German spies everywhere, Kell and Melville struck. Twenty-one German 'spies' were rounded up on the very day war was declared.

Some were executed by firing squad at the Tower of London. Although for Kell it was a major victory, there was a huge furore over the government's reprieve of a female agent. Kell and the Security Service argued that if the Germans thought Britain was soft on women, the Kaiser would flood the country with deadlier-than-the-male Frauleins.

By the time of the 1918 Armistice, K's empire had grown to some 850. Aided by a 'very experienced assistant' who was out on 'compassionate leave' from Parkhurst Prison, 'M' kept busy teaching new recruits the finer skills in life – like lock-picking, safe-breaking and covert burglary. In the 'Central Registry' – still there, only now worked by robot trains and screened behind armoured glass – he devised an elaborate card index with thousands of names for investigation. Each file was tagged, in an eccentric classification system that ran only from A–B. AA stood for 'Absolutely Anglicised'. AB was 'Anglo–Boche' (allegiance unclear). B stood for 'Boche', and meant hostile. If you were labelled BB – 'Bad Boche' then you'd had your sauerkraut. Ruth, MI5 and the *Spooks* registry still use a very similar system.

Secrecy was the by-word for both agencies, which were so incognito they weren't officially acknowledged to exist. Yet there were glaring holes in security. The London cab driver's joke was that every one of them knew where MI6 was – to the extent that somebody once painted a yellow line along the street pointing to 'C's comfortable Georgian front door.

By the Second World War, the Americans hadn't yet invented the CIA (Central Intelligence Agency), so it was the British Security Services that had to do battle with the SS intelligence arm, the Sicherheitsdienst – and the Gestapo.

In the police state of 1930s Germany, children turned in parents, neighbours shopped neighbours; anyone even suspected of disloyalty could be imprisoned or executed. In the UK, where the domestic front was relatively peaceful given the backdrop of the Depression, MI5 was slashed to a staff of thirty. The government saw Bolshevism, MI6's department, as the real foe. Official papers from this time vividly illustrate a life of pitiless paper-pushing for most MI5 officers. But for a lucky few, there was still glamour, excitement – and all the intrigue that goes with spying incognito on your own side.

OUT OF THE BOX
One of MI5's nicknames is 'Box', after its official wartime address of PO Box 500; its current address, PO Box 3255, London SW1P 1AE; and the fact that espionage reports used to arrive in special boxes. Until the 1990s, it was run from a series of blank-faced London buildings. Thames House, designed by Sir Frank Baines in 1928, was the Grade Two listed solution (*above*). Overlooking the Thames and only minutes from Parliament, it was once dubbed 'the finest office building in the British Empire'.

The 1990 estimate for its conversion was £85m, but some claim it was double that. Even the carpet in the staff restaurant was £70 a square metre. With squash courts, bars and a gymnasium, it is almost as glamorous as the 'Grid'. Desks are an ice grey; glass-roofed atria are used for meetings; the formal rooms have rich brown walnut panelling and deep purple and Prussian blue carpeting. A robot monorail protected by glass screens shuttles files and papers between the Registry and the eight floors above. Staff moved into the building in 1994. After the 11 September attacks in 2001 a new agency, the Joint Terrorism Analysis Centre (JTAC), was also brought in to work alongside MI5.

This was a world of 'bright young things' in which the diplomatic cocktail party still had a place centre stage. In a scene that strongly recalls Zoe's various femme fatale encounters in a silk dress (*right*) and stockings, a 'Mrs Barton', MI5 informant, records going to a party at Claridges. Her job was to spy on the mysterious suspected foreign agent known only in the official papers as 'Victoire'. There 'V' met Lord Selborne, the wartime minister for the Special Operations Executive. 'Lord S. may be merely playing up to her,' Mrs Barton 's report states tartly. 'But even if only half of what Victoire told me is true, then it seems he is behaving exceedingly foolishly.'

The Second World War brought excitement, glamour and a cast of colourful characters. Captain 'Tin Eye' Stephens ran the top-secret Camp 020 interrogation centre – a mansion on the edge of genteel Ham Common, London. With his 'tin' monocle, this inspired interrogator refined psychological intimidation to an art form. He had ways of making anyone talk – without resorting to violence. It was Stephens who unravelled the fiendish German plot to smuggle spies armed with deadly bacteria into the UK on a fleet of fifty fishing boats. In fountain pens ... Tin Eye made sure the germs stayed in Germany.

MI5 and MI6 were instrumental in winning the Second World War. The famous 'Double Cross' system – turning German agents back on the Third Reich – was crucial to the success of the 1944 D-Day landings. False intelligence, or 'chickenfeed', got the Nazis looking the wrong way. But as Harry says in *Spooks*, 'chop off one head of the hydra ...' Post–war, a new enemy emerged: Communism and the Soviet Bloc. One of MI5's main tasks was to stop the Red Menace from 'getting into' the army. Sixty years later, in episode 2.8, Tom Quinn is still dealing with the same potential problem.

The Spy Who Loved Me

The Cold War saw a frenzied period of spying on all sides. Recruited by the KGB at Cambridge University during the 1930s, turncoats Kim Philby, Guy Burgess, Donald MacLean, John Cairncross and Anthony Blunt inflicted huge damage on the security services. Philby, a charismatic and charming man who handed many a British or American agent over to torture and death, was even at one point considered as a possible 'C'. He betrayed almost all of MI6's anti-Soviet operations and gave Stalin all Winston Churchill and Harry S. Truman's plans to thwart the progression of Communism into Europe. The 'special relationship' that Churchill had so carefully nurtured was in tatters.

The fact that all the 'Cambridge Five' except Philby were homosexual might explain why, decades later, when MI5 officer David Shayler was being recruited, he was asked if he slept with lots of women. 'Chance would be a fine thing,' he joked. It was the right answer – if he'd been gay, he felt sure he would not have got the job.

Shaken, but not stirred...

Britain's reputation abroad might have been all but destroyed were it not for the efforts of one man – Bond...James Bond. The long and punishing war had left the country deflated, under-nourished and impoverished. At a time when Britain's empire was waning and its geopolitical influence was at an all time low, Ian Fleming's 'fairy tales for grown-ups' came galloping to the rescue. The books – and later the films – fed the world and a war-weary British public a diamond-studded diet of death-or-glory spying, glamorous girls and gorgeous gadgets that masked the reality of Britain's economic decline. And every time Bond got the girl, the British public was spared the shame of thinking about Suez. We could still punch above our weight – and, of course, below the waist.

It was sex that exposed the equally exotic life of real spies to an enthralled nation in 1963. More precisely, the three-way between Secretary of State for War John Profumo (*left*), a showgirl and a Soviet naval attaché. The Profumo affair – one year after the Cuban Missile Crisis brought the world to the brink of nuclear war – was the first major public exposure of MI5 at work. A good-looking toff from the highest of high society, the Harrow and Oxford-educated John Profumo fell for the lowly, but smokily sexual, Christine Keeler at Lord Astor's ultra-fashionable Cliveden country home.

It might have been just another affair – if Keeler (*right*) hadn't also been sleeping with Yevgeny Ivanov, the senior naval attaché at the Soviet Embassy. Keeler's friend Stephen Ward and her lover Ivanov both asked her to pillow-talk the future of Britain's nuclear programme out of Profumo.

MP George Galloway fiercely criticised 'the spooks' palace at No. 11 Millbank, with its lavish furnishings, its squash courts, marble staircases and chandeliers, its £25,000 climbing rock face in what was once a historic trophy room. He objected to the palatial conditions, 'none of which are enjoyed by humble police stations all over the country'.

The Spying Game

Through the 1960s and 1970s, spies were after all sorts of secrets. One Eastern European agent, known as 'The Chicken Tikka spy', spent many years and millions of roubles extracting the secrets of fast-chill food technology out of bemused British home economics specialists. But for others the game was still deadly serious. US Navy Warrant Officer John

A. Walker Jr., aka 'Johnny Walker Red' sold the KGB top-secret submarine data that cost the USA many millions of dollars and its technological edge. The world's top-earning double-agent, CIA officer Aldrich Ames dead-dropped his Russian controllers secrets brazenly culled from inside the agency's own Langley, Virginia HQ. Ten of the agents he betrayed were sentenced to *vyshaya mera* – being shot through the head and buried in an unmarked grave.

Plagued and provoked by their blatant espionage, in 1971 British Prime Minister Edward Heath expelled 105 Soviet personnel in 'Operation Foot'.

'...Known targets during the last few years have included the Foreign Office and Ministry of Defence; and on the commercial side, the Concorde, the Bristol 'Olympus 593' aero-engine, nuclear energy projects and computer electronics.'

By the late 1970s, MI5's resources were being redirected from counter-subversion work into a new concern – the growing threat of terrorism, not least from the Provisional IRA (Irish Republican Army), whose targets included British military forces, police officers, government and commercial buildings – and ordinary citizens. It was a bleakly terrifying period in British life. High-profile attacks like the 1979 assassination of Lord Mountbatten and the 1984 bombing of Brighton's Grand Hotel (which came close to killing Margaret Thatcher and her entire cabinet) made sure the covert war on PIRA stayed at the top of the agenda. MI5's counter-terrorist branch further grew with the rise of Middle Eastern terrorism: the massacre of Israeli athletes at the 1972 Munich Olympic Games; the 1980 Iranian Embassy siege in London. The SAS counter-assault that followed is the stuff of legend, and was vividly recaptured in *Spooks* episode 1.4, which sees Zoe taken hostage at the Turkish consulate and the theft of MI5's entire agent database. Now, there's one to keep Harry up at night.

MI5 and controversy
Fighting off KGB agents and Irish terrorists is one thing. But in many ways MI5 has been its own worst enemy. In 1985, former MI5 officer Cathy Massiter revealed that the agency had been illegally bugging politicians, human rights campaigners and pressure groups like the Campaign for Nuclear Disarmament [CND]. This rang lots of bells: Labour Party leader Harold Wilson had long complained about spooks working covertly to bring down his government.

The press sunk its teeth in, complaining that the catch-all provisions of the Official Secrets Act gave MI5 and MI6 too much power: the Security Services were out of control. Leaks began coming thick and fast, not least in *Spycatcher*, former MI5 officer Peter Wright's banned

account of his cloak-and-dagger, anti-civil liberty – and wholly unaccountable – life as a spy.

The veil of secrecy was gradually being torn. A House of Lords judgement in 1988 overturned a blanket injunction across all media outlets from reporting anything said by former intelligence officers. In 1989, the Security Service Act put MI5 on a statutory basis for the first time. Shortly after came a big surprise: the appointment of the first ever female Director-General.

Stella 'Rosa Klebb'

Back in the 1930s the novelist and ex-MI5 officer Compton Mackenzie had described the organisation as 'scores of under-employed generals surrounded by a dense cloud of intelligence officers sleuthing each other'. The service's reaction at the time was to threaten to sling him in jail. But after the Cambridge Five débacle, change was inevitable, if slow. Women were gradually being allowed to progress from secretary status, but the 'old boy network' and the class stranglehold on senior positions held firm.

By the 1980s, MI5 was well ahead of MI6 in trying to shed the Oxbridge-and-army-officer/gentleman's club image and recruit from an ever wider range of people. After all, the 'Cambridge Five' who had so damaged the services were recruited in the time-honoured tradition: by Blunt, a fellow at Cambridge. The organisation even started to use press advertising for recruitment, although the habits of secrecy die hard. In 1991, a young man named David Shayler answered a strange advert in the classifieds. It read: 'Godot isn't coming.'

'Very little comes to he or she who waits…move to a non-commercial organisation where an interest in current affairs is important. Where what also counts is your experience, your acute powers of analysis and your astute, practical common sense.'

The starting salary was between £16,500 and £20,500. 'No selling involved.'

Enigmatic? Just a bit. But this was a major change for an organisation whose Director-General would still attend official government events and not even give his name. Shayler would later go public with a new range of damning criticisms, and would be punished with all the weight of the Official Secrets Act thrown at his head. But in the nice-to-each-other noughties, the new appetite for openness was such that in 1993, the Major government decided to play its ace. There was now a woman at the head of MI5.

A single mother with two daughters, Stella Rimington was a straightforward middle-class girl from South Norwood, free from either a title or a military background. She did, however, have top links to the Civil Service through her husband. Recruited as a newly wed in India, Rimington spent twenty-two years working in the shadows – some of them running the Irish counter-terrorism desk. So the publication of her real name, her photograph and even her home address came as a huge shock.

She was being used as a political pawn by John Major's government, eager for 'good news' stories. But as yet, MI5 didn't do 'openness' well. The revelations enmeshed Rimington in a real-life version of an episode of *Spooks*, placing her and her family at huge risk, especially given her close past involvement with Northern Ireland.

FINE AIRS AND FACADES...
Built between 1927 and 1933 as a memorial to the many Freemasons who died on active service in the First World War, the Freemasons' Hall (*left*), where the *Spooks* team spend their fictional days, is a cavernous temple 123 feet long, 90 feet wide and 62 feet high, with marble walls and an extraordinary frieze. The 'Grid', the minimalist modernist interior of the series, is a studio set.

Portrayed in the press as a souped-up Rosa Klebb, in reality Rimington was a soft target, living in an ordinary private house in Islington, north London. When the media storm broke she had to run for it, young daughters in tow, to a hotel, living out of suitcases at a series of covert addresses until her safety could be guaranteed. She later told the *Daily Telegraph*: 'It wasn't my choice. I wasn't consulted. I was simply told, at very short notice, with very little consideration given to the impact it would have on me and the girls.' Her appointment marked a watershed: by the time Rimington became Director-General, fifty per cent of MI5's 2,000 employees were female, a statistic that holds broadly true today.

David Shayler, 'the renegade spy', was the next person to break the conspiracy of silence. His criticisms were many, but included a claim of inefficiency – for example the failure of a £25m IT system – and more seriously, examples of the real-life bugging and telephone tapping of innocent individuals and of a plot to assassinate Libya's President Gadaffi. He also claimed that MI5 should have prevented the IRA's Bishopsgate bomb in 1993.

Within two weeks of his first newspaper article Shayler was 'gagged' by an injunction and fled to France. The damage was done, though. This, along with the collapse of communism and the Irish ceasefire, added fuel to the loud calls for a scaling down of 'the newly idle hands in MI5'.

Meanwhile, the slowly rising tide of Islamic disaffection, both domestic and international was being largely ignored on both sides of the Atlantic. Yet the threat had been boiling up since at least 1983, when a suicide bomber drove a 400-pound truck bomb into the US embassy in Beirut, killing sixty-three people and wiping out most of the CIA's Middle East bureau.

A rising tide of anti-American, anti-capitalist and anti-globalisation sentiment was sweeping parts of Europe and the Middle East. The screw wasn't just beginning to turn – it was turning ever-faster. In 2000, suicide bombers packed a speedboat full of explosives and attacked the USS *Cole* in the Yemeni port of Aden. But the event that changed the whole world picture – and spying – for all time came on 11 September 2001, the eleventh anniversary of George Bush Sr.'s address to the UN calling for 'A New World Order'. On what came to be known as '9/11', nineteen Al-Qaeda terrorists hijacked four planes in the United States. They flew two into the Twin Towers of the World Trade Center in New York, a third into the Pentagon. The fourth missed its target when the passengers fought back. In all, 2,943 people died. Exactly 911 days later a terrorist attack struck Madrid, followed by the London bombings of 7/7 2005.

Not surprisingly, the Security Service is recruiting as fast as it can. Woefully unprepared through the 1990s, MI5 aims to have a strength of 3,200 by 2008. Its response to a world of terrorist threat, and 'the enemy within' has been to create a service that combines some of Vernon Kell's original principles with the overseas 'Station' structure set up by MI6 in the 1940s and 1950s: adding a regional structure that can put officers directly out in the field. Since 2005, MI5 has opened six regional Stations, and plans to open at least two more. A new 'Operations Centre' will soon be established, outside of London. The 'man from Uncle' could soon be 'the man from Doncaster'. Or Leeds, Newport, Skeffington or even Winterbourne Bassett . . .

Nowadays, at a time when 'invisibles' – British nationals who support or promote terror but can't be easily detected – can travel freely across the world, spooks work ever more openly. More than 3,000 Security Service records are in the public domain (although MI5 is still exempt from the Freedom of Information Act). An MI5 'telephone hotline' number – 020 7930 9000 – has even been given out so that 'ordinary members of the public' can report 'terrorists, spies and serious criminals'. Or you could always send them an e-mail . . .

THE CIA

The Central Intelligence Agency began life in 1947, replacing the
wartime Office of Strategic Services [OSS], America's first espionage and
covert operations agency. Its major responsibility – apart from making
Harry, Tom and Adam's life hell – is to gather intelligence – HUMINT, or
Human Intelligence; and ELINT, Electronic Intelligence, including spy
satellites and telecommunications intercepts. As Colin tells Danny when
identifying the double-dealing Oliver Mace with a massively enlarged
satellite image: 'I think it was taken from an American satellite.
Apparently, from that height, you can read the letters on the side of
a can of Coke.' As so often, Spooks was only a little ahead of its time.

The 'Company' has special powers under the Central Intelligence
Act: its director can spend agency funds without accounting for them;
the size of its staff is secret; and employees can be hired, investigated,
or dismissed without protection. It doesn't, though, have any power
to operate on the domestic front: to safeguard civil liberties, the Federal
Bureau of Investigation (FBI) runs US domestic counter-intelligence.

The CIA has often been criticised for heavy-handedness, and
especially for interfering in the domestic politics of other countries.
It was seriously damaged by failing to predict the terror attacks of
11 September 2001. In 2004, this once all-powerful institution became
one of several agencies subsumed in the $44 billion p.a. intelligence
apparatus overseen by John Negroponte, Director of National
Intelligence. In the UK, the Security Services' budget, shared between
MI5, MI6 and GCHQ, was published in 2004 as £1,296m. [Although some
commentators claim the true cost is £3bn this is still pretty small beer
compared to the Yankee dollars.]

In sharing much of America's awesome amount of raw intelligence, the UK enjoys a uniquely privileged status – one that successive British governments have been anxious to preserve.

America's new National Counter-Terrorism Center claims to have developed a highly classified database of 200,000 known terrorists, along with better communication and increased efficiency. But mistakes are still made. The Hamas victory in the 2006 Palestinian elections was dubbed 'a stunning failure' of intelligence. The Bush administration was totally caught by surprise, Secretary of State Condoleezza Rice told reporters. 'Nobody saw it coming...'

AND THIS IS WHAT MI5 SAYS ABOUT *SPOOKS*:
The BBC's *Spooks* is a slickly-produced and entertaining drama, but, like other works of spy fiction, it glamorises the world of intelligence. The nature of our work can certainly be stimulating and highly rewarding (as the show's strapline declares, it is not '9 to 5'), but the programme does not portray the full range of our activities, nor the routine, but vitally important, aspects of our operations which would not make such exciting viewing. Particularly unrealistic is the way in which the characters in *Spooks* regularly act outside the law in pursuit of their investigations.

The role of MI5
> To frustrate terrorism;
> prevent damage to the UK from foreign espionage and other covert foreign state activity;
> frustrate procurement by proliferating countries of material, technology or expertise relating to weapons of mass destruction;
> watch out for new or re-emerging types of threat;
> protect the government's sensitive information and assets, and the Critical National Infrastructure (CNI);
> reduce serious crime through assistance to law enforcement agencies;
> assist the Secret Intelligence Service (SIS) and the Government Communications Headquarters (GCHQ) in the discharge of their statutory functions;
> build Service capability and resilience.

'NOW PAY ATTENTION, 007...'

'If we have learned one thing from the history of invention and discovery, it is that in the long run – and often in the short one – the most daring prophecies seem laughably conservative. Arthur C. Clarke'

There are lots and lots of gadgets in *Spooks,* most of them made up by the writers and brought to a living-room near you by the art department. But science fiction soon becomes science reality, and just as the team has predicted reality in the storylines, many of the invented gadgets and technological advances shown are already becoming real.

GADGETS AND TECHNOLOGY

DOES THE FACE FIT?

That *Spooks* stalwart, face-matching technology is a case in point. This has been around a long time – early systems were used in an effort to track down the Red Army Faction [aka the Baader-Meinhof group] in the late 1970s. While the real face-matching systems haven't quite yet lived up to their early promise, in *Spooks* they work like a dream.

Face-matching technology is different to the advanced 'Photofit' software Malcolm uses to help identify vicious eco-terrorist Owen Forster in episodes 4.1 and 4.2. Using 'Photofit' (*right*), a trained operator like Malcolm helps witnesses reassemble the face they saw from a computer database containing thousands of facial elements. In the real world, as in *Spooks,* this technology works well.

Incredible though it still seems, face-recognition technology is fast becoming reality. Israel already uses biometric scanning to monitor movements along the Gaza Strip. Various airports introduced it post-9/11, and the UK's citizens will soon use it for their passports. The city of Tampa in the USA has installed cameras linked to face-recognition software in its late-night district Ybor City. It first used the technology at its 2001 Super Bowl: pictures of every baseball fan were taken as they entered the turnstiles, to howls of outrage from civil libertarians.

There are currently a lot of flaws in this technology: if your surveillance photo is taken in a combination of bright light and shadow, for instance, the computer gets confused. Similarly, any computer would find it difficult to match a surveillance shot taken from an angle to one on a database taken full face. The human brain – even a baby's brain – is far better at compensating for lighting, angle, or changes like a false moustache.

The technology is also as blind as a bat without a world-beating database: if there's no existing photograph, there's nothing to match. Which is why we should all be more careful about where we store our personal snaps. Once they have you on the database, you're there for

life – and you just have to hope the system never mistakes your face for an Al-Qaeda suspect's fizzog. Otherwise it's shackles, the bright orange jumpsuit and Guantanamo for you.

GADGETS

Danny frequently uses a pen that is not a pen – it's a camera. You can in fact buy such a gadget on the open market: a snip at around £1,200. Serb leader Radovan Karadic's bodyguards allegedly carried fountain pens that fired 7.65mm bullets when you turned the cap – just like the mobile phone gun the 'JJ' character accidentally fires in episode 2.7. Do we like the pens 'Postman Zaf' uses to pass secret info to and from Adam via dear old 'Aunty May' in episode 4.3? Yes, we do. We also admire the pan-European sound-and-vision Global Positioning Service tracking device Adam wears on the trail of wanted terrorist Yazdi in the next episode, 4.4 – and the similar one waitress Tash wears at Thames House in episode 4.2. By 2008 the Galileo project could mean that Europe's spymasters are no longer dependent on the USA's GPS system, and can develop even higher-tech tracking and comms devices of their own.

WEAPONS

In episode 2.6 it looks as if a microlight aircraft armed with a 'dirty bomb' may be on course to take out the British Prime Minister's residence, Chequers – and the President of the United States. The microlight turns out to be harmless, but Christine Dale and Tom Quinn were right to worry. For years, Palestinian fighters on the West Bank looked at ways of using microlights to get in under Israeli radar cover, hit a target and then run. In reality, just as in *Spooks*, it didn't work.

The dirty bomb is one of the newest terror fears for built-up cities: it would combine conventional explosives with radioactive material that could contaminate everything nearby. The main idea is to spread fear and panic: the radioactivity is unlikely to kill, but might in the long term cause cancer or other diseases. A dirty bomb is also highly disruptive, because radioactivity is so hard to get rid of.

Electromagnetic pulse weapons, or EMP devices, are different, but they have the same inconvenience factor in our modern techno-reliant society. The weapons emit a sudden high-intensity burst of electromagnetic energy. Any unprotected electrical equipment, and anything connected to electrical cables will be disabled.

THE REAL 'BIG BROTHER'

Surveillance – of all kinds – plays a key role in spying, as actor Rupert Penry-Jones discovers to his cost. 'Adam' hates filming in the 'Obbo' van: 'It gets hot and sweaty in seconds, and you're all crammed in. Really claustrophobic.'

The advent of surveillance satellites and CCTV – another *Spooks* standby – has revolutionised the art of watching (*right*). As with the stories, the fictitious technological wizardry on display in *Spooks* tends to be a few years ahead of the real world. In reality, CCTV monitoring is not continuous, even in theft-aware shopping centres, and it certainly isn't generally available to MI5 in real-time. That's genuine 'police state' stuff.

The computer software that will enable real spies to model the full facial features of a target photographed in part-profile and from several miles up in space may not be with us quite yet, but it's coming. This is how the Grid team rather improbably identify Oliver Mace as the man talking to a terrorist leader on a West Bank rooftop at the start of 3.3.

The use of camera- and sound-equipped fibre-optic cable is now routine: shoved through a tiny hole made by means of a silent, slow speed but powerful drill, the cable's intelligent nose allows you to see and hear what's going on in target rooms.

Then there is Echelon. A top-secret joint espionage venture by the USA, Britain, Australia and Canada, Echelon is the biggest global spying network in history. Run by America's National Security Agency [NSA], the UK's top secret GCHQ and other centres, Echelon is a satellite spy web especially equipped to eavesdrop on electronic communications. These big ears in space listen for 'key words and phrases' in all satellite and radio traffic; everybody's mobile phone calls; military comms; e-mails and almost all other forms of electronic messaging, including ULF. Mentioned by Harry Pearce in episode 1.1 and scary in its implications for what remains of our personal privacy, the rule of law, international relations and democracy, Echelon listens to just about everything we say, all the time.

In a separate and solo venture, in May 2006 America's National Security Agency owned up to logging and 'pattern-matching' all international telephone calls made from and received in the United States. Most Western governments, including those of the USA and Britain, also archive and monitor all Internet traffic, reading what they want when they want.

AND THEN THERE'S 'OLD-TECH'

Lock-picks, which have been around since pre-Roman times, feature heavily in *Spooks*. Fiona is an expert, but you get the best look at a pick when Zoe goes to do a bit of surveillance housekeeping at the Turkish consulate in episode 1.3. They are still used, but bits can snap off in the lock, and they can leave scratches and other unwanted traces that can give the game away. The most common lock is the pin tumbler: a range of pins inside it can only be moved when pushed in the right way and in the right sequence. Even this lock takes a great deal of skill to open, listening for the sounds that mean the pins have moved in the right way. Newer 'gadgets', like a device Special Forces use that winds the entire door away from the jamb, mean you can bypass the lock entirely.

THE 'WET JOB' – COVERT ASSASSINATION

Secret services have resorted to some very bizarre and unpleasant assassination methods over the years. One of the most notorious in modern times was the murder of Bulgarian writer and journalist Georgi Markov, in London on 7 September 1978. Highly critical of Bulgaria's despotic ruler, Todor Zhivkov, Markov defected to Britain and found work as a freelance radio journalist.

On his way into BBC Bush House, the broadcaster parked as usual in a car park near Waterloo Bridge, and climbed the steep stone steps intending to catch a bus across the river. Nearing the queue of people at the bus stop Markov felt a sharp, stinging pain in the back of his right

Bulgarian Umbrella
Issued by KGB, 1978

In 1978 the KGB used an umbrella like this—modified to fire a tiny pellet filled with poison—to assassinate dissident

thigh. Spinning round, he saw a man bending to pick up a fallen umbrella. Speaking in a strong foreign accent, the man said he was sorry, hailed a taxi and drove away.

It was Todor Zhivkov's birthday.

Markov caught the bus. The pain in his leg worsened and he collapsed outside Bush House. Rushed into hospital with a raging fever, he died three days later in terrible pain. Scotland Yard launched an investigation and the coroner ordered a post-mortem. Examining the strange 'boil' that had appeared on the back of Markov's leg, doctors extracted what they at first took to be the head of a pin. In fact, it was a tiny metal pellet. When scientists at Porton Down, the UK's Chemical and Micro-biological Warfare Establishment, placed the pellet under a microscope, they discovered it was hollow and pierced with two 0.34mm holes.

The scientists ran further tests. In January 1979, Crown coroner Gavin Thurston ruled that Markov had been unlawfully killed with 450 micrograms of ricin, one of the most lethal known poisons. Many years later, after the fall of the Berlin Wall, two former KGB officers, Oleg Gordievsky and Oleg Kalugin revealed that a top secret KGB laboratory known as 'The Chamber' had built an umbrella with a specially adapted tip that could inject a wax-coated, ricin-filled pellet into human flesh.

The incident is echoed in episode 3.5 – although it's done much more humanely – when Danny steps up to take the life of biochemist Eric Newland, a Brit developing biological weapons for the North Koreans. Danny injects Newland with insulin while he's asleep on a ferry crossing international waters: that gives MI5 total immunity. Nowadays, 'wet jobs' tend to be carried out by deniable 'contractors'.

Episode 1.2

TOM *takes out a big wedge of cheese.*
HELEN We're going for dinner, remember.
TOM Osborne's going to ply us with booze. So as long as your stomach's full of fats, it'll stave off the effects for a couple of hours. Tip from the top. Eat. Oh, also…when you drink, just wet your lips. Makes it last for ages. Come on. Tuck in.
HELEN If I get bad dreams, I'm blaming you.

THE TRICKS OF THE TRADE

The term 'tradecraft' covers a massive spectrum of activities – enough to fill a book of its own. And from almost the very beginning of *Spooks* we realise that there are many, many ways things can be fouled up. Drinking too much despite the cheese, and buckling under the stress of maintaining her 'legend', debutante spook Helen makes an error of judgement that sees her die in one of the grisliest – and most controversial – TV endings ever.

Sent to bug pro-life extremist Mary Kane's home, Zoe and the team |let the cat out of the bag – or in this case, the front door. The only way to get the pet moggy back again, so that Kane will not know they have been inside, is to get creative with the cat food.

EXT. cottage, Wirral – night.
ZOE keeps a lookout as PAUL jimmies the door. Opens it. A grey cat slips between his legs, and into the darkness.
PAUL Shit.
ZOE What?
PAUL I've let the bloody cat out. You never said there was a moggy in there.
ZOE Go check the kitchen cupboards. (*He looks blank*) …Cat food!
PAUL runs off. RINGO has now joined ZOE.
PAUL reappears with a saucer of dry cat food.
PAUL Right, that's dry kibble there, and I found some old tuna flakes in the bin, so I've sprinkled them on with a bit of olive oil, 'cos sometimes they like it a bit moist.
RINGO What the bloody hell's going on?
He goes inside. ZOE is left alone with the saucer. It starts to rain.

All new MI5 recruits undergo basic training at a secret facility inside Portchester Castle, a one-time Roman fort in Portsmouth, and now the site of a military complex. They are given basic firearms training, and introduced to the ABC of surveillance, counter-surveillance and anti-surveillance techniques, before going on for further training elsewhere.

Animals, especially dogs, are a serious enemy of covert activity: geese famously saved Rome from barbarian raiders. And goats compromised Gulf War I SAS mission 'Bravo Two Zero' – twice. *Plus ça change ...*

Possibly the best-known piece of spying tradecraft is the so-called 'dead letter drop'. It's a lo-tech solution to one of the knottiest problems in espionage: how to pass information undetected. At its simplest, the agent makes a pre-arranged mark on an object – say, a stretch of wall or a letterbox – that is on the subject's normal route to signal there is something for the handler in the box, or vice versa. The handler or agent then goes to the pick-up site – which will be as covert and innocuous as possible – to collect the package.

Lots of things – like children scoring random chalk marks or erasing the ones the spooks made – can wrong-foot this system. The mark, drop, or pick-up element may be spotted by the enemy – agents get very stressed and nervous – the package intercepted and everybody sent to jail. Or shot. Which is why some bizarre methods of covert transmission have been tried over the decades. In the 1980s, the spying community jumped on a bizarre new fashion for sticking toy models of the popular cartoon cat Garfield inside car windows. According to an MI6 source, British spooks in Moscow stuffed hi-tech data transmitter/receivers into standard issue orange-and-black stripy Garfields, and were then able to drive past palmtop-equipped agents and pass information unnoticed. Until, that is, the Russian Secret Service [FSB] did notice.

Think this is too wacky to be true? In 2005, the FSB filmed British spooks in Moscow lurking around a fake, fibreglass rock (*right*). When the Russians took the 'rock' apart, they found a battery-powered transmitter-receiver that could send encoded radio signals up to a range of 20m. Broadcast on television news stations across the world, this ham-fisted attempt at up-scaling dead-letter technology for the twenty-first century was a serious embarrassment to the four British 'diplomats' fingered for the rock job – not to mention the UK government. 'Q' must be revolving in his grave.

Asked to comment on the incident, Russian President Vladimir Putin said: 'Why would I want to expel these useless British spies? If I did that, they might send some new spies who were competent.'

Maybe MI6 would have done better to use a more tried and trusted method: the scytale, developed by the Spartans around 400 BC. Used for top secret comms by military commanders, the scytale was a tapered baton with a long strip of parchment wrapped around it. The secret message was written along the baton, one letter on each revolution of the strip. Unwrapped, the strip looked like scrap. But when the general at the other end wrapped it around a second, identical baton, the message was easily read.

Another ancient way of doing things was to write a secret message on a wax tablet, melt a second layer of wax over it and the write a boring, innocent-looking message on the top layer. Once the tablet reached its destination, the top layer could be scraped back to reveal the hidden message. Simple.

The best way to send material nowadays is by rapid-burst, encrypted radio signal from your laptop to the target laptop, preferably by secure military satellite. So long as the enemy doesn't intercept the transmission – and break the code ...

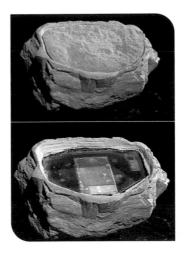

SECRET WRITING

The problem with invisible inks, as the Romans and early inventors like William Fox-Talbot knew, is that you can't see what you are writing: only when you warm it does the lemon juice message appear. The modern solution, according to former MI6 agent Richard Tomlinson, was discovered by total fluke. In the 1980s, a British technician working on a message posted from Moscow wiped the back of the envelope – where the real message had actually been written – with developing fluid. A second script, written in a different hand, suddenly emerged on top of the original. It was just an ordinary address. But it was back to front ...

The technician realised another envelope must have been pressed up against the original and the address – written in what had to be an ordinary, commercially available ink – had invisibly transferred itself. This could be gold dust. MI6 mounted a massive search. It turned out that the mystery super-pen was the Pentel rollerball.

JUST TO BUG YOU

To keep a closer eye on right-wing racist Robert Osborne [episode 1.2], Danny and the team manage to bypass the ferocious countermeasures Osborne has in place, only to leave a telltale fuse on the floor. Real covert entry teams make a detailed photographic record on the way in, and use the shots to check they have left everything inside the target premises exactly as it was.

They also have a buddy-buddy system, like divers, to cross-check and prevent mistakes. You have to be methodical to the point of being downright obsessive: most teams have all their tools and other pieces of kit numbered, labelled and fitted into custom-built cases to minimise

the risk of leaving anything behind. And covert entry teams always have what's called an 'actions on' or contingency plan in case the subject heads home unexpectedly. A back-up unit, for example, might 'accidentally' crash into their car, holding them up for a crucial twenty minutes.

Teams will often take up the floorboards, insert a bug beneath, nail everything neatly back in place and re-lay the carpet. They can do this much faster than you would believe possible. On one such operation, bugging two top IRA members in Northern Ireland, Special Branch couldn't understand why they were getting such a muffled signal from the bug. Finally, it dawned. The suspects, a man and a woman, were cooking up their nefarious plans in the next-door bedroom – in between bouts of bonking. The Special Boat Service [SBS] – the UK's surveillance experts extraordinaire – had to go back in and insert a second bug in a tiny hole drilled up under the bedroom mantelpiece. This time, they got the juice.

In *Spooks* you often see low-level surveillance in teams of two. In real life, although the optimal number in a surveillance team is around a dozen, many more of MI5's dedicated 'A' Branch watchers may also be tasked to follow a top-priority target. Teams on foot would be 'squaring the block' – i.e. rolling in a moving wave along the subject's projected route. They will follow them, but sometimes also lead them, with pre-positioned watchers at strategic points like tube stations and bus stops. The Russians are reputedly the best at this: an immaculate operation follows 'Moscow Rules'. Instinct is crucial: 'If it feels wrong, it is wrong.' Flexibility is key.

Teams also use vehicles of every description and place watchers in stakeouts, including overlooking houses or garages. These properties will have been bought, or wangled out of their usual occupants by cunning means, like the 'free holiday' trick Sam employs in episode 3.3. Covert photography is key for information and identification, but it could also be used for prosecution. It is the speciality of MI5's A3 and A5 branches, rather than a stray spook with a telephoto lens.

One of the best examples of surveillance and anti-surveillance work in *Spooks* comes in the same episode, when Adam Carter, in a memorable tradecraft duel between massed ranks of MI5 and MI6 watchers, treats us to a fascinating lesson in anti-surveillance techniques – diving into buildings and transport hubs without notice; changing clothes and re-emerging in a different guise; and, in a classic 'choke-point' gambit to expose his tail, crossing the Millennium Bridge. The bridge is too long, too thin and too exposed for someone to go unnoticed by the trained eye. Ideally, Adam would follow an agreed route devised by MI5 with watchers stationed precisely to detect a tail. At one point, Adam confuses his watchers by donning hooded sweat gear and joining a team of rowers. But the old ones are sometimes the best ones – it's

Harry's neat variation on the 'sliding doors' tube train trick that foxes Adam's MI6 tail – and chief ghoul Oliver Mace – in the end, successfully 'clearing his coat-tails'.

GARBOLOGY

Around such tiny things as the trash a whole story can turn, and the writers of *Spooks* have been doing their homework. In the very first episode, pro-life extremist Mary Kane exposes her weak spot when the *Spooks* discover a positive pregnancy test in her dustbin. Plenty of real-life spies have rued the day they forgot to put their garbage through the shredder – or at least roll it up and eat it. Top US agent Katrina Leung, code-named 'Parlour Maid' was arrested in 2003 along with her lover, former FBI agent James J. Smith, and put on trial after investigators found compromising documents shredded in her rubbish. The USA had paid the Chinese American $1.7m to collect intelligence about China's military capabilities: it would have been very upsetting to find she was a double-agent. Leung was acquitted, to huge sighs of relief.

In 1979, CIA agents in Tehran spent hours and hours shredding vital secret documents in the days before the US embassy was overrun and captured. Strip by painstaking strip, Iranian students reassembled them. The lesson was learned: sensitive material must be burned.

In October 1993, an industrious FBI 'G-man' stole the trashcan from outside CIA double-agent Aldrich Ames's house. A computer printer ribbon inside it showed that Ames had written to the Russians. This gave the FBI the evidence it needed for a covert search. Ames had made another serious blunder: upgrading his word processing program, he didn't realise that the new system automatically saved copies of his old documents. Every word he had typed to the KGB was still there. Ames got life in jail.

Even innocent-seeming documents like discarded ration requisition forms can give clear evidence of troop strengths or movements, and the amount of personal information – phone numbers, bank statements, compromising cards from friends or lovers, political affiliations – that can be discovered by rooting through the rubbish is something that today's spooks and fraudsters have seized on with glee.

LO-TECH

Hounded MI6 spook Richard Tomlinson records clandestine night-time trials of a top, top-secret weapon: a mouse. Trying to bug a suspected Russian agent in Lisbon, a British MI6 station secretary rented a flat several floors below his penthouse. But setting up a radio link to connect a bugging device with the recording equipment in her flat proved impossible. The trouble was that a wire needed to be threaded all the way through a fiendishly convoluted system of pipes. The rickety Portuguese building defeated the spooks at every turn – including the various *Mission Impossible*-style crawling devices the Malcolms among them invented. So they decided to use a standard issue mouse instead.

Three mice agents were recruited: Micky, Tricky and Thicky. Micky was a natural, crawling his way through the antediluvian central heating system of trial site Century House like the daredevil he was. Tricky was okay, bar the occasional 'incident' when he would chicken out, and try to climb back up his fishing wire. Thicky was a dead loss, so Micky and sidekick Tricky were flown out to Portugal in a Hercules to complete their mission. Now retired from active service, they live in a safe house somewhere in Britain – with as much cheese as they can eat for life.

WE HAVE WAYS OF MAKING YOU TALK . . .

Both Adam and Tom have continual problems with interrogation, Tom memorably getting nowhere with Harry's young burglar JJ (*right*), who simply walks out on him [episode 2.7]. Wartime MI5 perfected an interrogation technique that did not resort to beating, bullying or Nazi jackboots.

The top secret Camp 020, run by the monocled Captain 'Tin Eye' Stephens, was an interrogation centre within a genteel Victorian mansion. It was Stephens' work that unravelled the dastardly German plot to use biological weapons against the UK: deadly bacteria, hidden inside pens and pencils. The pen was always mightier than the sword . . .

The mansion, on Ham Common, was modified to stop inmates speaking to each other. Listening devices were placed in cells and pipes buried within masonry to prevent prisoners tapping Morse code.

A few quiet days would be followed by an all-important first interrogation with up to five officers, 'impressing the prisoner with the hopelessness of his own position and the omniscience and omnipotence of the British Security Service'. If the suspect refused to capitulate, he or she would be shown typewritten obituaries of 'executed prisoners'. (Torture by reading . . .)

As a last resort, prisoners would be put in solitary confinement and have the daily ration of three cigarettes removed . . . Time and again, this softly-softly method seems to have worked.

Nowadays, as we know, prisoners are routinely hooded; shackled; roughed up if not beaten; deprived of food, water and sleep; put in 'stress positions' like Robert Morgan; kept naked and hosed with freezing water. And, if all else fails, in the case of US prisoners, 'rendered' to a third country where the security services can and do use any method they please to extract information without anyone in an American uniform – or for that matter, business suit – getting their hands dirty. Spying is a dirty game, and some of the things you may find yourself involved in can rest on your conscience – forever.

THE
WRITE
STUFF

'The star of *Spooks* is not us actors. It's the script. Peter Firth (Harry Pearce)'

'It sounds very basic, but "stuff" has to happen.' Ben Richards was a young novelist and first-time screenwriter when he started working on *Spooks* – and the production team helped him see the light. *Spooks* isn't just pacy: every single episode delivers a narrative right-hook, or else it |just doesn't make the cut. 'Stuff', or good, old-fashioned storytelling: that's what puts bums on sofas. Richards hardly knew what had hit him.

The *Spooks* team trusts its writers – sometimes even to the point of allowing them on set. But they have to fight like cats in a sack to get their stories made in the first place. To a degree, *Spooks* has adopted the American writing model of the 'brainstorm'. The show's writers, directors and producers spend three days in a Cotswolds hotel talking. Then they talk some more, covering the essentials like what's going to happen to the characters so they develop through the series. The writers then – very informally – make bids for their scripts, using the ideas that were strongest and that survived all the scrutiny. But there the similarity with the American model ends: once the rough episodes have been agreed, and the producers have worked out the order they will come in, the writers are left, pretty much without interference, to get on with it.

A full script takes about three months to get 'from 0–60' as series creator David Wolstencroft puts it. 'But things change all the time: actors aren't available, or you might have to push something else forward. It's often as much the budget as anything: if you've specified shooting on a canal boat and that boat alone is going to cost £60,000, you might just have to say goodbye to that scene.

'That's what TV writing is. It's not about getting "your play" on, in the way that you fondly imagined. It's about getting the story down as well as you can within the practical limitations. But that's also why when TV is good it's very, very good: I'm not talking *Spooks* here, I mean in general. It's because you have these limitations: that's where the art comes in, rather than throwing money into blowing buildings up.'

Award-winning *Spooks* writer Howard Brenton thinks there is only one real spy story: the story of the double-agent. Who's telling the truth, who's lying, who can or can't be trusted? Many episodes in *Spooks* ring changes on this basic plot. Adds Brenton: 'The thing with *Spooks* was always to "spend" story – spend, spend, spend it. Jane [Featherstone, executive producer] would often give me this horrible note – "Well, Howard, this is a terrific script. Now why don't you start with Act 3? Just move all that right to the top."

'Makes you want to pull your hair out. But that's what you learn – don't make promises. Just deliver the story, right up front. That is one of the reasons why the series has such directness.'

HEADLINES AND HARD HATS

Packed with detail, the firecracker-fast scripts often take inspiration from a newspaper headline. 'The real world is now, of course, scarier than any book, because it's actually happening to us,' says Wolstencroft. 'It is OUR story. That's the way it is for spies, only worse. Once you look at the world like that, it changes you. Professionally sanctioned paranoia seeps into your after-work psyche.

'As far as the writing goes, simply stating the threat is not enough to engage people's imagination. The threats already exist: it's more about lifting the whole thing out of documentary reality. Life has become larger-than-life. So, we have to go one step further.'

'It's a magpie thing – things you hear on the news, things you store up because you are interested in them. Anything can spark you off,' adds Ben Richards. 'With the two-parter that starts series four, I'd been reading about cults that believed the human race need to be culled. This eventually became the 'Shining Path', a mix of the Tokyo sarin gas cult with some extreme Animal Liberation Front thrown in. At the same time, Kudos wanted to have an episode that was a race against time – to discover that there was a bomb, deal with it – and then realise there were nine others.'

Sometimes it's only a detail in a real story that gets turned around and used to spark off a new idea. 'For instance,' says Wolstencroft, 'I noticed a tiny story about some storage tanks around Sellafield that got refurbished . . . It just got me thinking.'

This was to become episode 1.6, co-written with Howard Brenton, the cliffhanger which nearly saw Tom, Ellie and Maisie (*left*) blown to kingdom come – a good example of how the writers worked together on ways to 'make the political personal'. This might sound a bit airy-fairy, but it's a key mantra for *Spooks*. For us to care whether Tom, Adam or Harry lives or dies, the job of the writer is to put the maximum pressure on them as people. Then the characters are used as 'plot drivers'. If his 'old enemy' – the IRA – was involved, then an emotionally damaged Harry might lose perspective and start making bad decisions. Likewise, Tom's job is eating him alive. He doesn't just take the work home – he takes a bomb. In a sense, they are one and the same thing.

'Most of the straight information driving the 1.6 plot,' says Wolstencroft, 'came from the Internet. An Irish website was complaining that Sellafield, right next to the Irish Sea, wasn't well enough protected. They singled out the thickness at the top of the storage tanks as a problem. When we discovered a missile with a "top attack mode" that would pierce a metre of concrete, we knew we had a story.' It was another of those times that MPs got hot under their collars about *Spooks* because the material was so close to home. Called 'Sefton B' in the script, the nuclear facility was in fact 'a thinly disguised Sellafield, which is in an isolated position, is very near Ireland, and if it were successfully attacked would be a total disaster.'

TAKING RISKS AND TALKING THEATRE

Spooks stands out because of its willingness to experiment. Just as, on the acting front, the show helped stars Hugh Laurie (*right, top*) and Tim McInnerny move onwards and upwards from their *Jeeves and Wooster/Blackadder* comedy typecasting, it has also brought on new writers and directors and cultivated the best in other fields.

Top playwright Howard Brenton came into the series almost by accident, having written a play for RADA about Christopher Marlowe, the Elizabethan playwright and master spy. Executive producer Jane Featherstone asked Brenton if he would like to try a screenplay, 'for fun'. He ended up writing around half of the first series and much of the next.

Being able to call on a writer with a background in theatre gave the *Spooks* team the opportunity to experiment. In episode 2.5, Tom's mettle is tested to the limit in a so-called EERIE exercise (*right*) – when he has to shoot someone on his own side. The situation, familiar to fans of Jean-Paul Sartre, is very theatrical. Compress the action into a small, closed space; put the characters under intense, ever-increasing pressure – and watch the drama boil over.

For Nicola Walker [Ruth], the experience was only too real: 'When we did the read-through the director Justin said "I want you all to treat this as though it were a piece of theatre – a play. So learn your lines in advance." If you've worked in the theatre, where everything is done in sequence, that's a treat...Soooo, we're locked into this one set for two whole weeks. The first couple of days were great – but by about day six, everyone started to get a bit twitchy. By the end, when it's revealed that it's a test rather than an actual situation, the look on all of our faces when the lights come up was really telling. We all look exhausted – and green...We did a lot of – "bonding" might be the term.'

'We called it "Grid Hog Day",' remembers Shauna MacDonald [Sam]. 'We were in the same studio, the same room all the time. And it was very, very hot. The air conditioning wasn't working, and the huge lights were on for so long...everything deteriorated on the Grid as things got ripped apart. It was like doing a marathon, as much as a play.'

'Originally intended to save budget, the EERIE exercise turned out to be more expensive than they had realised,' says Brenton. 'The designer was dead unimpressed, saying: "Why didn't you tell me at the beginning of the series that you wanted all this wire and stuff and holes in the wall? We would have built it in." But I didn't know I was going to write it like that beforehand.'

When Brenton's son joined Imperial College, London, the

playwright's imagination travelled back in time to the Elizabethan theatre. 'I was thinking of a Faustian plot: what would happen if, twenty-four years later, having won a Nobel prize for science, you suddenly found out that you owed your glittering career to MI5? Suddenly Harry is standing there. It's payback time.' This became the notorious 'Red Mercury' episode. The police turned up on Howard's doorstep (a bit of a novel departure for a playwright, even though Brenton is no stranger to controversy), asking him how exactly to make 'Red Mercury'. The substance is an international, as opposed to an urban, myth – what Brenton calls an 'Inter-myth.'

LAST THOUGHTS

Suspense, suspicion and swindlers. *Spooks* shows us the new Britain, one where image and spin are the ultimate rulers. Its plots are unsettling and challenging precisely because they are so close to life. The series has cropped up in Hansard, the record of UK parliamentary debate, no fewer than ten times. Which for a fictional television series has got to be a first.

The show really got under the skin of MPs. Prompted by their previous night's sofa duty, they raised all sorts of sticky spy-type questions. What is happening to the privacy laws in this country? How much phone tapping actually goes on? Was the BBC whipping up too much controversy about race? Are all IT 'geeks' always men? Is *Spooks* better than *Heartbeat*? Well, I guess we all know the answer to that one: try looking *Heartbeat* up in Hansard ...

It's Kudos' insistence that writing is all that has brought the show thus far. Unlike many television shows, the writers are encouraged to use their brains – just as long as the 'story stuff' still happens. The team are all very different, with their own obsessions and convictions that lead their imaginations under the very skin of the state, and into the psyche of the would-be terrorist. Perhaps MI5 should consider putting them on the strength?

'We might be journeymen writers,' says Wolstencroft, 'but there's nothing in our imaginative power that makes any of us a terrorist mastermind. Rest unassured, whoever is putting together the next catastrophe is far beyond us ...'

Thanks, David.

WRITER PROFILES

David Wolstencroft

The original creator of the series, Wolstencroft did not contribute to series four or five ('my mother gave me a note') because he was writing two novels and scripting *Shooting Dogs* – a film on the genocide in Rwanda. He loves secrets, and his bedside reading matter includes the likes of Graham Greene, John Le Carré, Len Deighton, Robert Littell and David Morrell, author of *Rambo*.

Q: Why are you interested in spying?
It's more just people really. The thing with *Spooks* that really grabbed me was the idea of somebody who had to be an extreme person because of their profession: lie, and run different identities and feel that they are really at the business end of national security. You could get into extremely difficult situations and emerge victorious or not – and then have to go home. To face that 'moment' with your partner – 'well, how was your day? – well, fine ...' That sense of the emotional currency  of secrecy intrigued me.

Q: Do you have a favourite character?
Ummm ... I always love Zoe very much, and I love Malcolm.
   Tom was the favourite to begin with, and the challenge was finding an actor who could portray someone with about a million gale force winds going on behind the eyes, without actually showing anything. When we found Matthew that was just wonderful.
   In terms of always being the common factor in every series, Peter Firth has done some fantastic things with Harry. And I think he is the most quotable character.

Q: Is Harry intended to be a 'chorus', in the classical sense?
I just think he's a linchpin. You just know so much has happened to that person to get to that position. It means that you can bring things up with his past constantly, and have fun with them.

Q: The density of the scripts marks *Spooks* out. Are they really difficult to work up?
Extremely, because they are basically movies. They have as much story as a ninety-minute movie, in my opinion. I've almost seen *Spooks* as 'espionage rep'. You have these stories to tell. If you were telling these stories as stand-alone movies you'd have to set up all the characters and their relationships and so on. Whereas in *Spooks* we basically start twenty minutes into the movie. They are story monsters, those episodes. The challenge is to make the characters' emotional universe truly compelling, at the same time as telling the story. And you don't do that

by doing a scene with the 'personal', and then a scene with the 'professional'. You do it as all story and all relationship, all of the time.

It can be very difficult to get right – and it's very intensive.

Q: How does the team work together, and how do you create a 'brand'?
With Kudos and Howard and Simon Mirren we worked very hard to really establish a strong character for the show. And that brought a lot of people in, wanting to write for us, and they already knew the characters. So that's what I mean about it being a bit like rep – we would have these story meetings (the extreme American model would be to put everyone in a room for forty-three weeks of the year: we just go home after a few days). Jane Featherstone would project-manage the creative side as well as the production side. It's the Holy Grail to be able to do that. She's not a writer, she's more of an enabler, but she has a very, very good story sense. You can't learn enough really, about the production side: also how to cut things out, too. This might be a typical conversation: 'This whole sequence David, where people are jumping from canal boat to canal boat . . . we need to film most of it in a tiny confined space – can you make that interesting? And anyway, that canal boat is going to cost us £60,000. We have £100 . . .'

Simon Crawford Collins has taken the lead now, to really say: 'Here are the ambitions for the series, and this is what the BBC liked about the last one – now here are the ways that the characters could go.' And there's a lot of very bright, talented people around the room, so the idea spins off in all different directions. All of that's recorded and distilled into ten episodes that may work. And then everybody goes off and starts to work and then get scripts commissioned. That's when problems or conflicts may emerge, and we sort them out. That is the challenge: you are trying to communicate not just what happened but also the significance of what's happened to the director, the cast and everybody. And that's where [director] Bharat Nalluri's skill and wizardry came in, initially, too. He worked to create this really individual look. We were always trying to break the speed limit, do things that no one else is doing.

Kudos have been amazing in that they have really locked down the overall look of the show since then, with different crews and directors.

Q: What's most fundamental to that brand?
An ability to take risks. We factored in the fat fryer thing from the beginning. [Star Lisa Faulkner, playing Helen, was murdered in only the second episode.] The cavalry doesn't always come. There is a perception of the thriller show that the principal never dies. So there's often not that much narrative tension. The reality for spies is that they sometimes intersect with parts of society that really are horrendous. The risks can be extremely high. And it had to be intelligent – you can't make a stupid show about the intelligence service.

Howard Brenton

Author of some of the most trenchant and poetic lines in *Spooks*, Brenton's roots are actually in the theatre. Fond of satire and knock-about black comedy, his plays include some of the most controversial in living memory. *The Romans in Britain* of 1980, a parable about British colonialism, provoked violent protests. Brenton's vast experience as a writer has been useful in pulling *Spooks* out of plotting pitfalls, and he wrote both the series one and two 'cliffhangers', whose resolution needed a lot of careful handling.

Famous for mould-breaking plays like *Pravda* (co-written with David Hare) and *The Romans in Britain*, Brenton may almost be as well known now as the man who wrote 'Tom Quinn' [Matthew McFadyen] out of the series. A left-wing paper once described Howard Brenton's *Spooks* episodes enthusiastically as 'anti-institution TV'. But he doesn't see it that way. Brenton may know all about moral responsibility and rebellion – when he was a boy, his policeman father turned Methodist minister and upped sticks in dramatic fashion, moving from comfortable southern England to Ebbw Vale. But like David Wolstencroft, it is the psychological landscape within the secret state that the playwright is most interested in.

Spooks has given him the chance to write about some of the themes that interest him most: disillusionment, deceit and despair (think rogue agent Angela Wells in 4.10, the last of series four). When he and Hare wrote *Pravda*, they were setting out to write *Richard III* in Fleet Street. Writing *Spooks* has given him free rein to explore a vast range of cultural inspirations that roam from ancient Arabic texts (2.2) via the theatre and *Faust* (3.2), through to ground-breaking films like Carol Reed/Orson Welles's *The Third Man* (2.10).

Q: What interests you about spying?
There's only one spy story, really. It's the double-agent – the person pretending to be something they are not. The question is: are they who they say they are? Someone is always having their veneer cracked. There is something in the actual genre, the alienation of the spy story that pushes it towards an anti-institutional, anti-establishment line.

Q: How big are the differences with the theatre?
There was always the assumption that we could create complex stories for *Spooks*. The main difference is this thing about heroes. The theatre is built on anti-heroes – Jimmy Porter, Richard III, King Lear. They are all anti-heroes. Also, heroines like Hedda Gabler, Lady Macbeth – all villainous or deeply flawed. That's even true in comedies. But in popular television there have to be true heroes. How to write a hero – how to make them interesting, as well as good – has been the big dramatic education for me.

The neat plot line which David set up in the first series – of Ellie not knowing Tom was an MI5 officer and that he was already living under a false identity with her – was a wonderful set-up. That would always be resolved, though, because we couldn't show him in a bad light. You can't trash the hero – you need him next week. Always, if there's any, not to say friction, but discussion between you and the producers, it is when they worry you're showing him in a bad light.

Q: So were you in your element when Matthew McFadyen decided to leave the series?
I really rubbed my hands together, yes! If an actor begins to think of Hollywood, it's the writer's big chance. Your natural drive is to write stories about failure, because failure is more interesting and easier to dramatise than success. It was great – Tom becomes a real human being again. He just can't 'double life' himself any more.

Mind you, Matthew McFadyen did wonders. He could give the character a depth that wasn't there to start with. His line might be 'X-ray Zero out', or something, and he'd say it with some edge of suffering that was hard to put your finger on. We were advised by former intelligence men. When you meet some of them, what strikes you is those hard eyes – the temperature in the room dives by ten degrees.

Q: Why did you choose to write about the death of Princess Diana? [episode 4.10]
I was fascinated, not so much by the conspiracy theories about Diana's death, but at the hold they had on the public imagination. There are hundreds of theories. The Internet is crawling with them. A very cruel middle age was probably awaiting Diana, but the tragedy allowed us to reinvent our dream princess.

Q: Any funny stories?
Sometimes there are budget problems. At one point the team said, 'We must do an episode abroad. Would you like to write it, Howard, as a special treat?'
   'Yes, please.'
   'Where would you like to set it?'
   'Istanbul...'
   'And?'
   'Vienna,' I said, off the top of my head. So my first draft starts with a murder in an Istanbul souk. There are all these great visual sweeps of backstreets and beautiful mosques, and then the action moves to the streets of Vienna. After all that, when it came to it, they didn't have any money. Istanbul turned into a Tottenham alley. And I think a second unit, which is basically the director with a camera, went to take a few shots of the blue mosque in Istanbul and that was it. They cheat

wonderfully, of course. There was one scene, set in the desert with people firing guns off into the night and a hawk and a tent. That was done in a car park in Islington. It's extraordinary what they can pull off – the dream machine is so adaptable.

Ben Richards

Widely travelled in South America and unhealthily obsessed with General Pinochet, Ben Richards has written a number of novels, including *The Mermaids and the Drunks*. He was a rookie screenwriter when he first came to *Spooks*, but has now become a key member of the team. Richards has the distinction of being the writer who 'killed off' Danny and (sort of) Zoe. His plays include *The Case of the Blue Oyster Gang*, a spoof private eye thriller.

Q: What's been the best thing about writing for the series?
Most writers' ideal would be to have people sitting around in rooms having intelligent, witty conversations. The problem is, while that's great for the writers to flex their muscles, it's not so great for the audience. So writing for such a plot-driven series was a very good training for me. I've learned a lot from it, and the more blurring between genres the better, as far as I'm concerned. You have to think about writing for an audience and not be too self-indulgent about it. And you realise that there's nothing vulgar about 'things happening'.

Taking me on was definitely a risk: the first couple of scripts needed a lot of work and they were very patient. We went through what felt like countless drafts. Kudos is very writer oriented. They didn't panic – or at least they didn't show me any signs of panic!

Q: Do you enjoy watching the shooting?
It's incredibly boring. When I was a smoker I'd work my way through around eighty cigarettes per shoot. I get phone calls from set sometimes. I know the actors reasonably well and quite often they'll either phone, or the script editor will ask what did I mean, or how do you pronounce something. Sometimes an actor will ask is this line really consistent with my character? I always give in, because I'm weak and star-struck. Seriously, though, I'm always quite happy with that ... there are some lines that look better written down than spoken. If you come from a literary background you have to watch that.

Q: What themes interest you the most?
I like spy films but I didn't have a driving desire to write spy stories. In Keeley Hawes's [Zoe's] exit I was interested in the moral ambiguity of her situation. She did some things that were wrong, in fact illegal, but you could understand why she acted as she did. But what really interests me is the balance between security and civil liberty.

I am interested in the idea that Britain could be sliding towards totalitarianism, and we test ideas to the limit by taking the themes out to an extreme. A few years ago if you had somehow known what Al-Qaeda was going to do, you would probably have been met with mass disbelief. But once you get that Maoist fervour and combine it with the easy availability of some very dangerous technology, you have a massive problem on your hands.

Q: What's the funniest thing that's happened to you on *Spooks*?
We have to include a lot of 'tradecraft'. In the very early days, I wrote a scene in the pub with a ferret. It had cameras in its eyes. Which I thought was an inspired idea … I was rather proud of it. But the ferret was very quietly cut. It remains a running joke between us. I keep trying to slip in a ferret in one form or another – in the dialogue, or into the action – but they always notice. And they always cut it.

Rupert Walters

Rupert Walters started his film career playing an Oxford student in the TV adaptation of Evelyn Waugh's novel *Brideshead Revisited*. He went on to write films that include *Sisters* and *Oxford Blues* and worked for many years with top Hollywood director Michael Mann. He joined the team later than the others – to date, he has written three episodes for *Spooks*, and is currently writing for series six.

'Although the serial elements have to stay the same – the characters and the setting of the Grid – you're quite free to write about ideas and stories you're interested in. I like the idea of being provocative, taking on issues that are murky, using a story to investigate them. It's not *Panorama* – more the stories on the edge of the news.'

Q: What themes interest you the most?
I was interested – without going so far as John Le Carré's 'moral equivalence' idea – in the extent to which we in the West may, or may not, be responsible for why things have gone wrong. Dramatically it makes a better story if you can turn events in on your own side. If it's just a case of, 'Oh, it's the guy over there in the shamag', then that's it – the story's over.

Episode 3.3 has the old idea of MI5 and MI6 fighting each other – but the question of competence underpins that. They keep saying they can't tell us about their successes, about all the bombs they have stopped from going off – but right before the 7/7 bombings in London they lowered the alert level, which suggests – means – they weren't on the case at all.

The duality where one lot of spies has a completely different agenda from the other interested me – the idea that simply moving about a city could be kind of scripted, every move pre-planned. When you squeeze that into a drama, it's amazing stuff.

The other thing that intrigued me was that whole notion of how a spy walks down the street – the complexity of hundreds of people watching one suspect. One intelligence guy told me about working in China, where nobody has ever run an asset because they'll put the entire block onto you – 800 people. Unlike Danny and Zoe outside the target's flat: just the two of them, and he's at the heart of a dangerous anarchist cell.

And then there's secrecy. The official 9/11 report concluded it was secrecy that actually let them down. Had the different agencies not been so secretive about what they did and didn't know, the attack might not have happened. To be sympathetic, with the size of their problem it's difficult to decide what really is a threat – and what's just people sitting round in a café talking tough, who are never going to do anything.

I was also interested in interrogation in a general sense – how do you get stuff out of people? Is beating them effective, or not? They do say that in certain situations – if they need to get the information by Friday, say – some of the Middle Eastern agencies don't bother. They just bring in your family and start shooting them, one by one. You have to be pretty tough not to speak under those circumstances. I was interested in the extremes of that: how low would our side sink to stop an outrage? The answer is, pretty low.

Q: How well or badly did you feel that reflected on Adam?
The idea that Adam had been through torture was based on William Buckley, the CIA station chief in Beirut who was tortured and murdered in 1984–85. He was strung up in a house in the Beka'a valley. He knew everything and I don't think he lasted long. It made me feel, if they catch you, then you may as well just tell them what they want to know. Strangely enough, everybody felt that Adam needed harder edges at that point in the series – and after he went as far as he did with the Robert Morgan character it felt like he had a different weight. Unless there is something in the present the characters are acting out, back story is very difficult to establish. A kind of ruthlessness came out in Adam: when he had to go there, he went. And we went with him, back into his past. There isn't always much room for exposition in *Spooks*.

Q: Any regrets?
I read a story in the papers that one of Salman Rushdie's bodyguards was shot in the hand by an Iranian diplomat when Rushdie was close by. Rushdie was a liberal, anti-Thatcher figure who in the end became very close to the guys looking after him, most of whom probably voted for her. He had a real emotional and political metamorphosis in that time, when he realised these 'coppers' were putting their lives on the line for him. I should probably have done more with that, but with television there's a limit to how much metaphysics you can include!

THE
CRYSTAL
BALL

ENEMY WITHIN – HANDLE WITH CARE

Spooks vaults the barrier between fiction and reality. At the very heart of its success lie uncanny foretellings that even the cast and crew find chilling. 'You almost start to worry about receiving a script, because you don't know what's going to happen in the real world,' says Rory MacGregor [Colin]. 'You read it and then two weeks later, the same thing happens.'

Riding a wave of fevered interest in espionage post-9/11, in 2002 the series punched its way into the real news. The shattering episode 1.2 – the chip fryer murder – was about a repugnant right-winger deliberately creating havoc in the UK by smuggling in illegal asylum seekers. There were no final credits after the music, so viewers dived straight into the nightly news bulletin. The top story that evening? The crisis on asylum seekers.

Where do the writers get their information? Could it be that the team has penetrated right to the very heart of the real MI5? 'Some of the writers must have very good sources,' adds a still-unnerved Rory. 'We rigged a casino roulette wheel once. Then days later we read in the papers about a gang ripping off £1.3m by doing the same thing ... Oh dear.'

But it can get stranger than that. When the 'Section B' team was forced into an EERIE (an Extreme Emergency Response Initiative Exercise), the simulated nerve gas attack on the UK's major cities became one of the most intense pieces of drama ever written for television. Ironically, this shining example of ensemble acting was mainly budget-driven. Sticking to the Grid for an entire episode would, it was hoped, save precious money. But as they were filming, the news came out that the capital was staging a real-life 'remount', as it is known in the security world.

'It was amazing to pick up the newspaper and read about the real exercise,' says Keeley Hawes [Zoe], 'when we had literally shot scenes just like that the same morning.'

This unerring nose for the next 'big story' has intensified throughout the series. In episode 1.5, a corrupt former government minister mixed up in illegal arms trading finds God in prison. This comes close to the wire, faithfully and memorably echoing disgraced minister for defence procurement Jonathan Aitken's 'simple sword of truth' speech. But at least that was something that had already happened. Whereas, when the news about torture in Iraq's notorious Abu Ghraib prison broke, the cast and crew had just finished filming a script by Rupert Walters examining whether torture can ever be 'legitimate'.

In a powerful and claustrophobic drama written a full year before, Danny becomes more and more disturbed as Adam interrogates mercenary Robert Morgan (*left*). He seems to have taken to heart Elizabethan arch-spymaster Robert Walsingham's dictum that 'violent diseases must have violent remedies'. This snatched bit of conversation between Sam and a surprisingly unconcerned Ruth tells us just how far Adam is going:

RUTH The human ear is most sensitive to that exact pitch. So it drives you slowly insane and can lead to complete hearing loss.
SAM Isn't that called torture?

Surfing the breaking news wave has its problems. In episode 2.8, where a military regiment is about to mutiny (*left*), the story was, as usual, grounded in reality: serious grumblings about the British Army's pay and conditions. The problem was that – quite unintentionally – both the script and the costumes identified a real-life unit that kept cropping up in the news. 'We had to re-shoot two days of footage,' says David Oyelowo [Danny]. 'It meant doing it all again, only with slightly different lines and different costumes – confusing, but part of the excitement, as well.'

You really know something's good when it starts making the news, not foreshadowing it. The *Spooks* team's willingness to challenge, to test and to tackle awkward issues has made the headlines time and again. We've seen it swamp MI5 with thousands of eager new recruits (first series), and then frighten them away in case they meet a violent death (third series). In the wake of rows over the BBC's impartiality, the Hutton report and the manipulation of intelligence before the second war in Iraq, *Spooks* has continued to raise real leading questions. Does the government want 'the nightmare of a Ministry of State Security – our very own KGB'? That quote from Harry Pearce prompted the *Daily Mail* to ask: 'Could the fictional plot have been actually hatched by MI5 to express its fear for the future?' Er, not really.

In 2005, author Ben Richards' opening two-parter 'Surreal World' (*left*) for series four was so controversial that BBC head of drama Jane Tranter agonised whether or not to air it. Written and shot months before the dreadful 7 July attack on central London, it, too, featured deadly terrorist bombs causing mass civilian casualties. The villains were nihilist extremists rather than an Al-Qaeda-inspired cell, but the similarities were still shocking.

'We actually had a line in the two-parter in which, post the first explosion, someone said "the PM's flying back from the G8". But once 7/7 occurred and the PM actually did fly back from the G8, we got spooked ourselves, and removed it,' says assistant producer Katie Swinden. Other than that, it survived uncut, but BBC continuity announcers warned viewers in advance that they might find the drama disturbing. They were right.

And then there is the whole intermingling of the political and religious agenda. With religion once again an 'opium of the people', *Spooks* has examined the subject long and hard, with episodes exposing the violent side of American 'pro-life' evangelism, and the suborning of Islamic youths by extremist preachers.

Never one to take the easy route, in 2002 writer Howard Brenton decided to tackle the hot issue of the Finsbury Park Mosque...

Free speech and fair comment: The Birmingham Mosque episode

> **Many people will be happy, jumping up and down [after 11 September]. America is a crazy superpower, and what was done was done in self-defence. Abu Hamza.**

Screened on 9 June 2003, this episode was so topical it hurt. Nearly eight million people tuned in to watch when *Spooks* dared confront the conspiracy of official silence over what was happening inside some of Britain's mosques.

The context: a Britain crackling with racial tension. Egyptian-born Abu Hamza al-Masri (*right*) had been ousted from the Finsbury Park Mosque in February and stripped of his British citizenship in April. In June the far-right British National Party (BNP) won eight council seats in Burnley; violent race riots had raged in Bradford and Oldham the summer before. The programme had had its first outing the week before on BBC3. This gave the vociferous PC lobby time to launch a campaign. The BBC received 500 calls from people who had heard about – but not seen – the programme and were 'concerned'. Kudos producers Gareth Neame and Jane Featherstone were besieged by emails.

As the controversy played out in the tabloids, Muslim groups insisted the BBC was being irresponsible. To her great credit BBC1 controller Lorraine Heggessey refused to take the episode off the air. When it went out on BBC1 only 150 people actually complained. Perhaps this was because Tom, Danny and Zoe had shown us, only too clearly, something we all feared might really be true.

Challenging it may have been, but 'Nest of Angels' was dreamt up to be as much an exploration of good, as bad. Says Howard Brenton: 'I actually wanted to write a story about a good Muslim. He would be against what was happening in his faith and take enormous risks to stop it. But of course this is a Western drama, which is a dialectical form. Therefore you must have a bad Muslim, too. It's at the root of the way we think in the West: for every protagonist you must have an antagonist.

'Although you couldn't say so at the time, because of the libel laws, there were bad men in some mosques, so my antagonist became an Abu Hamza-type figure. Ibhn (*left*), an Algerian academic and super-agent, offers his services to MI5. Yet his position is left ambiguous. It is by no means clear that MI5 will even offer him permanent residency in the UK.'

Brenton, whose plays for the theatre include the searching *Paul* and *In Extremis*, knows his stuff when it comes to religion. He has also travelled widely in the Middle East. He admits that you can get into a 'liberal tangle' when dealing with such a highly charged subject. But he is adamant: 'You have to wrestle with the difficult things. Too hot to handle? You just have to say bullshit to that.'

FROM 'NEST OF ANGELS': THE MULLA 2.2

RACHID What is it to wear a hundred and fifty pound American trainer shoes? To put on jackets with a label from Milan in Italy? What is it to drink alcopops, to go clubbing and end up fumbling a slut of an English girl on a canal path in the dawn, your mind wrecked with pills? It is nothing but ash in the mouth, the taste of the death of the soul. For the West sells you the illusion of an earthly paradise. It has to, that is how American Jews on Wall Street make their money. But despite all the pressure of the West's gaudy promises, in your schools, on the television, in the cinema, the way your British friends behave, even the advertisements in the streets, you have kept yourselves pure. You have become the West's worst fear: young people they cannot sell to, that they cannot touch. You know the way to the true paradise, through a martyr's death. My young brothers, I envy you.
A silence.
Then he stands and everyone in the room is on their feet, eyes blazing, fists shot up into the air in ecstasy on the word 'death', as they shout a chant in unison.
ALL Death to America and her allies!

In the meantime, *Spooks* hadn't just prefigured the news bulletins. It *was* the news. Birmingham's Central Mosque was defaced with the slogan 'Suicide bombers inside – kill the bombers'. Reports – never proven – claimed that after the programme young Muslims were being beaten up by white thugs. But Brenton and the Kudos team were unassailable: 'Nest of Angels' preached tolerance, not violence.

IBHN The Prophet himself – peace be upon him – wrestled with demons and angels, Abu. There is no shame ... The only paradise we will see will be one we make on earth, Abu.

THE
HARDWARE

THE GUNS

❝ When in doubt, have a man come through the door with a gun in his hand. Raymond Chandler ❞

Guns on television. Tricky in a world where real violence is on our screens every day and there's so much of it. Simon Crawford Collins, *Spooks* executive producer, has this to say: 'Ultimately, we want to make intelligent drama, but there's no two ways about it – we all like seeing people jumping through windows and helicopters whizzing over cars.'

Too right, we do – and we also like seeing people using guns; big ones with extra menacing twiddly bits and long barrels. If we didn't, then we wouldn't be watching a ballsy, hard action show like *Spooks*.

Thrillers thrive on weapons, and *Spooks* gives us everything from the basic flick-knife Joe Kennedy tries to stab Professor Curtis with in episode 4.2, to the Sidewinder-armed Harrier GR4 fighter-bombers called in to protect the Prime Minister's home, Chequers, against a possible terrorist flying in by microlight in episode 2.6.

Other hardware that stands out from the gun rack includes: the Gepard sniper rifle Herman Joyce uses to frame Tom Quinn in episode 2.10; the silenced Skorpion machine pistol the hitman in 3.3 sprays around the bookshop [a silenced version really does exist, however much Malcolm might raise his eyebrows at Danny]; and the Barrett-Browning .50. This fearsome tool of the sniper's trade is used to kill the terrorists about to fire a 'top-attack anti-tank weapon' at Sefton B nuclear plant in episode 1.6. Shot on location at a disused conventional power station in Kent, the weapon we see on screen is a LAW 90, as used by the US, British and many other armies. The LAW 90 fires horizontally but can slice through a foot or so of armour plate. We also see IRA splinter cell commander Patrick McCann with a hand grenade.

But it's in the upcoming series five that the SAS v 'the baddies' gun battles really explode on screen: the terrorists get to play with the awesome Ingram MAC M-10, heavy as hell but utterly devastating at close quarters. Spewing out 1300 rounds per minute, it's like working a lethal shower-head. For pistols, the latest set of *Spooks* bad guys tend to favour the Czech CZ-75.

'When we're using guns on a production like *Spooks*, angles are critical,' says stunt co-ordinator Andy Bradford. 'If you point a gun – even with a blank cartridge directly at your target, especially if you're

Skorpion

aiming at the head or chest area – you could maim or kill someone. It's critical that you put them with an armourer, show them the gun and how to be safe with the gun. On camera we make it look like you are pointing at the target, but in reality you are pointing just over the left shoulder.'

As for the boys in black, they get the spanking new HK UMP-9 sub-machine gun; the HK MP-5 SD [this one is silenced]; the HK MP-5KA4 [does the Increment love Heckler & Koch? Does it ever]; the folding stock Colt M16A1 and its M203 grenade-launching variant; the standard issue Glock-17 and the Beretta 92D pistols; and that new favourite with US and NATO forces, the Barrett-Browning goes-straight-through-a-breeze-block .50 sniper rifle.

Ingram MAC M-10

THE ARMOURER'S TALE – FAUJJA SINGH

'My main job,' says Singh, 'is to help work out safe angles of fire, and also where to position the grip, the dolly, the tracks, the actors, the soundman and the camera team for maximum visual effect. And at the same time maximum safety. Then you've got to get everyone to stay there – especially the actors. Bearing in mind that with almost all weapons, the hot, spinning, dangerous spent cartridge cases eject slightly rearwards to the right, you have to try and make sure they fly behind the actors and crew, not hit them. A cartridge case can smash a dinner plate at two metres, so you don't want one hitting you in the eye. All weapon types have roughly similar habits when it comes to ejecting spent cartridges. But then, each individual weapon has its own idiosyncrasies that have to be watched and learned.

CZ-75

'The real problem comes in when people start to move. This massively increases the risk of someone getting a hot cartridge case in the face. With a shotgun, there is the problem of the wadding blasting out of the barrels – and most people don't realise that even standard blank ammunition blasts hot gases and powder debris out to a range of at least two metres. Getting in the way of that can blind you – or worse. So my stomach's always churning on set, in case one person does something they shouldn't.

'If you go into an old building with a lot of loose, flaky plaster on the ceiling and walls, or a lot of dust and rubbish on the floor, you have to project what will happen when the firing starts: fragments can go in people's eyes, dust goes over the camera, there's a lot of potential for concussion and there's the fire risk – plenty to think about. If there is a lot of firing or it's taking place in a very small space, the grip wears a facemask, goggles and gloves, the cameraman and focus puller wear a fireproof blanket and everyone puts on ear defenders.

HK MP-5K

'We had one set-up where we were firing guns at a sewage works surrounded by stinking raw sewage. Lovely. There was a real risk all that methane would go bang, and that would have been us finished. We had to bring in a massive battery of fans to keep the gases blowing in the opposite direction.'

The weapons

'We chose the Gepard for series two/three because it's reckoned to be the best sniper rifle for shooting someone from a distance of one mile – and because it looks the business.

'Every director has his or her own point of view about which weapons to use. But after series two, the producers, directors and cast got together and decided that since the real MI5 uses it, from series three onwards our *Spooks* would carry the Glock-17 pistol, standard issue for the UK police, including Special Branch and SO19. MI6, on the other hand, routinely uses the Sig-Sauer 9mm.

'On the James Bond film *Die Another Day*, the director wanted a small, snazzy pistol Halle Berry could carry on her upper thigh, and that hadn't been seen on screen before. Took me ages to fit the Beretta Cheetah on Halle, for some reason – all fingers and thumbs. We used the Cheetah after that on *Spooks*.' In series two, Tom Quinn and Danny both use a Beretta 92F – would James Bond approve?

SIMPLE IS BEST
'We had one scene (episode 3.6) where a guy comes straight into a building and shoots somebody. And we did that very simply. We could have had blood spattering all over the walls for effect — but we just didn't need it. He doesn't even get up from his chair. As the bullet hits him the chair just goes back and you see him hit concrete. Wonderful. We put what we call a "fall pad", a four-inch pad behind the chair, pad the subject's elbows etc. and tell them not to throw their head back.'
Andy Hay, director episode 3.6

A DAY IN THE LIFE OF THE SPOOKS CREW

What's it like being out on a typical day's shoot with the *Spooks* team? Like being part of a small army dedicated to one thing: visual and narrative brilliance. Not so small, either, this particular unit is some fifty-strong. Easily outnumbering the loud milling crowd of passers-by, the crew are filming a delicate, covert exchange between traitor 'Neil Sternin' [Matt Day] and terrorist 'Sharaf' [Dhafer L'Abidine] for series five, on London's Millennium footbridge.

It's a sunny summer's day, and with the Tate Modern soaring on one side and the shapely, gleaming dome of St Paul's Cathedral on the other, the river sliding steel-grey below, this is a location to die for. Except for the joggers, that is, whose thumping footfalls make the camera bounce and spike the sound; and the tourists who stop to watch and take pictures of the *Spooks* unit, er, taking pictures. Mums and Dads with pushchairs stray close to the cables and the masses of tangled but valuable gear. The homeless man would like a bottle of water.

Dedication; focus; single vision. Everybody's at it, from director Andy Hay to floor runner Sarah Brand, doing a great job of keeping the unit as one. It's going alarmingly well, despite outside interruptions. The actors deliver their lines on cue, the camera, sound and art direction teams are on the case. Costume, make-up, lighting, everyone's professional, ice-slick and there are no dramas – except the one they're trying to get in the can.

How did it get like this? When a film unit turns out TV this good, it's a lot to do with knowing where you are going: the set-ups and shots, how you get the best out of them, fast. And that comes from the top. Andy Hay's easy-going, unruffled style belies a crystal-clear vision of what he wants – which everyone agrees makes all the difference. Behind him, the producers, who insist that story and production values stay right up there at the top of the television tree with the likes of *CSI* and *The Sopranos*. And let's not forget the writers, who will keep on turning out those future-seeing, gripping scripts. Then there's always a core of people in the team who have been here before, many times before: through series two and three, and in the case of carpenter Laurie Griffiths, way back into the mists of that first, unforgettable series.

It takes roughly twenty-seven days, plus two or three 'second unit' days, to create each episode. When they get a bit of spare time, Andy and the photography director will do a few hours getting shots to use

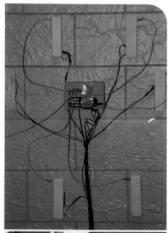

as 'time lapse' – speeded-up shots. They will then put together some of what the Americans call 'general views'. It'll give the audience something solid to hang on to. 'The scripts are already very complex, and I hate films where you don't know where you are,' Andy explains.

Job done on the Millennium Bridge and we're packed up and back to the big, sprawling *Spooks* Unit Base over by Tower Bridge. Lunch is as good as always, from the caterers or catering truck: beef curry, veggie spaghetti Bolognese or seafood gumbo; salads, bananas in rum, coffee and tea, the works. Food to fight on and, if you're part of the *Spooks* team, you need it. This is hard, hot, demanding work.

The unit take a couple of pick-up shots inside the terrorists' car, 'hands and legs', then move on to the day's major business. The scene being filmed involves our baddies having six blocks of explosive wired at the heart of the Saudi Trade Centre (*left, top*). Oddly, the blocks are in the shape of a rough cross, with a red detonator centred in the middle.

The clock's ticking, the SAS are on their way, but it's Ros Myers [Hermione Norris] who finds the bomb. She shoots it a horrified look and turns to run. Too late. The terrorists are on her, armed, intent and in her face. Ros/Hermione tries to explain: 'Sorry, I was just looking for the ladies ...' but gets slapped to the ground. Another take, then another; take three and Andy's happy. So is Hermione who can finally get off the floor.

GRAB A GUN

The 'SAS' arrive, and armourers Rob Grundy and Ken Garside have a few treats in store for them. How about a silenced Ingram MAC M-10? – 1100–1300 rounds per minute. It 'works like a chocolate bar,' Ken says, 'everybody gets a bit.' Very nice, but no thanks. The MAC's a baddie weapon, but here's something: the HK UMP9, the latest Heckler and Koch sub-machine gun (*left, bottom*) – a seriously, worryingly beautiful design, so fit for purpose it makes you want to pick it up and use it.

Or how about the HK MP5KA4, with, 'ambidextrous, four-position trigger unit and optional red-dot/laser sighting'? A nice folding stock Colt M4 with Surefire weapons light? A Beretta 92D pistol? A couple of spare magazines? Not that we're getting excited here ...

Ken teaches the actors how to hold the guns – don't tilt the head to either side, a good, solid, stable stance. Balance is everything: front foot planted forwards, butt pressed hard back into the shoulder, lean into the weapon or it will lean into you. Don't look over the gun, or to one side. Get a sight picture, that's what the sights are for. This is the cocking lever, this is the safety catch, and this is the magazine release catch. If you pull that, the magazine flies off and you look about as much like an SAS man as a soft broom. It sounds easy, but it isn't.

Mossad bad-guy Simon Kassiandes explains: 'It's all about your body language. Plus, I now know the detail. If I don't stand at an angle to Dhafer [who plays the even badder baddie, Sharaf] when we are both firing an automatic, I would get hit in the face by the shells … and that would look stupid.'

Now for the big bang: the construction crew have built a claustrophobic, bilious green-painted set inside one of the big Unit Base sheds. Lighting supremo Mark Thornton and his team have it well lit; designer Robert Foster and stand-by art director Ben Barrington-Groves have made it look alarmingly sinister and real; camera and sound are ready, the actors are at first positions. Over to Ed Smith, of SFX GB, who has to make the blast live up to expectations.

The 'Semtex' – shaped biscuit foam – is glued to a pre-cut pearl-board, 'breakaway' wall. Each block is packed with as many old-style photographic flash-bulbs as it can hold, producing a super-brilliant flash like a real bomb when they explode. The blocks are detonated by 'mini-maroons', a pyrotechnic device made of magnesium and black powder. The whole rig is wired to a 24-volt two-button ignition board.

Ed positions five 'air mortars' behind the wall to make sure they blast directly at the watching camera – not to mention us. Loaded to 110 psi, each mortar has a solenoid valve-operated diaphragm that releases all its pent high-pressure air out in one hit when triggered. Just like a real shaped charge, the blast is directed by cones. In this case they are packed with all kinds of debris: lightweight bricks; bits of cork; vermiculite; balsa wood; cardboard and dust, like the real rubbish that comes flying at your head when a bomb vaporises inside a building.

The terrorist walks past in shot; there's a two-second pause, and then, kaboom! We're all mighty glad we wore the regulation ear-defenders, while the second camera team emerge grey, covered in debris, and brushing dust out of their hair.

FUN, OR WHAT?

Had enough yet? Not quite: one more sequence to film. The Increment, the men in black, looking very like the real thing in coveralls, black helmets, anti-flash balaclavas, nylon webbing, Glock-17s in open holsters, goggles on and guns at the ready. They steal in. Who'd want to be a terrorist now? But somehow top bad guy Sharaf gets away. Never mind: it's 6:30 and that's a wrap for the eleven-hour day. Strike the cameras, stow the gear, saddle up and head off for some R&R. Adam and the Increment will catch Sharaf tomorrow, in the tunnel shoot-out, just down the road. Maybe.

'Do the work,' Martin Scorsese said. On the *Spooks* unit, day after day, they do.

THE
CHARACTERS

WHO THEY ARE AND WHAT THEY DO . . .

TOM QUINN – MATTHEW MACFADYEN

Tom Quinn – strong, silent Tom, in many ways the copybook male: feels deeply, finds it hard to talk with the lovers in his life. Very much his own man. Which can work for you: through much of series one and two, Tom is the sheet anchor, the operational bedrock of the Grid team: calm in a crisis; resourceful; decisive; quick-thinking; persistent and steely in resolve. But even for Tom, the wormwood of living the lie does its acid work: leads to serial heartbreak; a crisis in confidence; and then terminal rejection of the double standards spying routinely demands. When nasty Jools Siviter asks 'Do you do ambiguity, Tom?' His answer is straight: 'No. Either a thing is a lie or it's true.' That might be, as Siviter says, an admirable point of view, but it's one that makes it difficult for him to survive in the shadow world of *Spooks*. Set up in the mother of all set-ups, distrusted by his friends and ultimately dismissed from the service, Tom suffers horribly. In a sense he suffers for us all.

Matthew is a self-confessed John Le Carré spy thriller nut. He began his acting career on the British stage, and has gone on to films, playing Mr Darcy in *Pride & Prejudice* alongside Keira Knightley. In his latest film, *Death at a Funeral*, he will again co-star with Keeley Hawes [Zoe], now his wife.

ADAM CARTER – RUPERT PENRY-JONES

From the moment Adam swashbuckles onto the Grid, we know the impossible has happened: not only is he a replacement for brilliant, tortured Tom, he is Tom's equal. Adam is good at doing the male thing of 'leaving a part of yourself in a box': which is why he's so competent undercover. Cool as you care, Adam's seamy MI6 background battling Syrian intelligence chiefs not only turned him into one of the savviest spies on the block, but won him 'gorgeous' wife Fiona. Strong-minded, ruthless and ready for anything, Adam is the Grid's safest pair of hands. Until Fiona gets shot dead.

'Adding or subtracting to the team takes a lot of thought. We want any new addition to be shining from a different part of the sky,' says series creator David Wolstencroft. In the character of Adam, they certainly achieved that. As the newest recruit to the fictional MI5, Rupert Penry-Jones was conscious of joining a well-established team both on-screen and off – although he already knew some of the existing cast. 'I'd worked at the RSC with David [Oyelowo], knew Matthew and had worked at the National Theatre with Nicola [Walker]. I don't think Adam starts out thinking he's going to be part of the gang, he doesn't try to do that. Coming into the show I felt like an outsider. Adam's the same. The cast were like a family, and so were the characters. I was the new boy, and it felt like that in the scripts, too.'

Although Rupert has played an on-screen spy before (*Cambridge Spies*), *Spooks* represented a completely different world. 'An officer could be walking along discussing a life and death situation and people are all around, going about their normal lives and oblivious to it. In the same way, when we're filming and doing a long shot, I'm maybe walking over a bridge surrounded by hundreds of people, and they have no idea what I'm doing. There's that feeling of separation, and reality becomes surreal. It's as though our characters escape into the real world, you're not really part of society.'

Gaining extra depth as the show goes forward, Adam definitely belongs now – and may even go on to become one of its longest-serving cast members.

HARRY PEARCE – PETER FIRTH

For much of the time, Harry hovers slightly above and behind the action, summing things up for us with trenchant lines. Which is not to say that he will not step in to sack the likes of traitor Tess, or Tom in psychological meltdown mode. The head of Section B, counter-terrorism, Harry doesn't always get things right – which boss does? But the difference with Harry is, he's wise enough to let his deputies influence – and often override – his own judgement. Headhunted from the Army, Harry's past is rich and complex enough that something plucked from it – the death of a friend in Northern Ireland; a past lover or an estranged daughter – can help make a good episode even better.

'Harry is the character that grew the most, really,' says Howard Brenton. 'We would always over-write Harry: give him tired witticisms and sub-Oscar Wilde dialogue; weary and back-handed comments. The producers were always knocking that out, because that made him look too cynical. But it gradually accrued, and Peter [Firth] began to really inhabit the character. He looks cuddly, but he's got a heart of stone. He's damaged himself and made a pact that he will live with the damage.'

The long-running gag is Harry's crossness and inability to deal with the younger generation. 'They all – the younger members of the cast – view me as the butt of quite a few jokes.'

HARRY Something's wrong...
RUTH How do you know?
HARRY You knocked.

Like Jenny Agutter, Peter Firth was a child actor. And like her, he starred in Peter Shaffer's *Equus* (both on stage and on film), which involved extensive full-frontal nudity. 'I feel I know Jenny as a best friend,' he says. 'That's what happens when you spend a long time naked together!' One of the beautiful people of the 1970s, Firth has played leading man roles ranging from *The Picture of Dorian Gray* to Angel Clare in Roman Polanski's *Tess*.

HARRY Do you understand atomic theory? Quantum mechanics?
DANNY No.
HARRY Nor do I. I don't understand politics, either.

ZOE REYNOLDS – KEELEY HAWES

The beating moral heart of *Spooks*, Zoe's integrity and honesty are beyond doubt. Her willingness to question – and even refuse – those little 'necessary' spook tasks like extra-judicial killing is one reason we find her so likeable. And why she is so close to Tom. Even when she takes Tessa's £10,000 bribe, we suspect it's only because her loyalties are torn. In the end, Zoe makes the right choice. Expert at undercover work, a great all-round performer on the Grid, Zoe's fall from grace mirrors Tom's: an operational error of judgement, coupled with the poison pill for relationships that is the life of a spook. Having made the only too human mistake of getting scared – very scared – undercover, Zoe becomes the victim of a frenzied, media-led government witch-hunt against the 'unaccountable' MI5. Luckily, Harry has an ace up his sleeve and she is niftily 'swapped' for someone else. Last seen on a veranda in Chile, sipping a cool glass of Merlot with 'is-she-really-going-out-with him?' snapper boyfriend Will.

In her own life actress Keeley Hawes is no stranger to controversy, having left her husband of five months for *Spooks* co-star Matthew Macfadyen. Previous roles in series like *Tipping the Velvet*, a story of a Victorian lesbian affair, have also excited the tabloids. She has now replaced Jonell Elliot as the voice of gun-toting Lara Croft in the world-famous Tomb Raider computer game and will soon appear in the film *Death at a Funeral*.

DANNY HUNTER – DAVID OYELOWO

Blessed with a sharp technical brain – but lumbered with a bit of a chip on his shoulder – surveillance king Danny's fluency with money makes him a believable undercover City trader. But money almost proves his downfall: too much in love with it, Danny succumbs early on to the temptation, as do Tessa and Ruth, of using the job for personal gain. Falling foul of Harry's all-seeing eye, Danny has to cut up his ill-gotten credit cards. Crisis over, Danny becomes what he's always so desperately wanted to be – one of the best. Quick-witted, brave and fiercely loyal, he comes in from the cold. But when the unremitting pressure crushes hero-mentor Tom, a devastated Danny turns away from 'I'm with Will now' Zoe, the love of his life. He bravely takes the bullet for Fiona, becoming in death the hero he has always wanted to be in life.

'What does it do to your humanity to be someone who just lies for a living?' Oyelowo asks. 'We wanted to show that spies are people, ordinary people in extraordinary circumstances.'

The son of a newsagent on London's Holloway Road – who was also a Yoruba prince – David Oyelowo is used to leading a double life. Visiting Lagos with his family when he was six, David discovered that his father had not been pulling his leg: the boy who lived in a two-bedroom London flat was officially escorted to the family compound on 'Oyelowo Street' by motorcycle outriders. In London, the other black kids called him 'coconut' – black on the outside, white on the inside – because he was hard-working and ambitious. So when Danny arrives at the Grid feeling a bit of an outsider, the real-life David has been there and done that.

David's rags-to-riches story was crowned when he became the first black actor to play an English king – Henry VI – for the Royal Shakespeare Company. In real life he is close to co-stars Matthew Macfadyen and Keeley Hawes – a bond that was strengthened by the tabloid storm that broke on their relationship.

HELEN FLYNN – LISA FAULKNER

For the *Spooks* producers, Lisa Faulkner was one of the show's biggest-ever casting risks. A tabloid favourite who starred in *Casualty* and *Holby City*, Lisa was first talent-spotted at a tube station at the age of sixteen. She also appeared in the 1996 drama *And The Beat Goes On* with co-star Jenny Agutter.

Hiring lovely Lisa got *Spooks* lots of headlines and previews, which was good. The problem was, they were going to kill her. In the second episode. 'It was quite deliberate,' says *Spooks* producer Stephen Garrett. 'We wanted to make it clear this was not a soap.' Which makes Lisa one of the most memorable short-lived characters in TV history. Lisa has gone on to star in *New Street Law* and *Murder in Suburbia*.

RUTH EVERSHED – NICOLA WALKER

If Tom Quinn suffers for us all, Ruth is lonely above and beyond the call of duty: so much so that she uses official surveillance data for a spot of personal stalking. Engineering a key meeting with the stranger she has set her heart on, Ruth stays single when he fails to make the kiss. Seconded from GCHQ, Ruth's loyalties are a little too easy to divide until she sees where her best interest lies: on the Grid, with the team, fuelling operations with incisive, well-sourced, learned and sometimes brilliant research and analysis. She's intense, over-sensitive and emotionally challenged – and probably doomed to a home life in Ealing watching classic movies.

'She's always been very interesting to write,' says Howard Brenton, who first introduced her as a character, 'because she's like a queen spider in the middle of an enormous web.'

Ruth is played by Nicola Walker and the part is so finely drawn that you are quite surprised to discover the actress is remarkably different from the on-screen Ruth. For example, while fearsomely bright (she began her acting career in the Cambridge 'Footlights' at university), Walker still gets alarmed by the braininess of what she sometimes has to say. 'When you get the huge chunks of information, a part of you dies,' she says. 'The fear, the terror, of not getting those lines right...'

As actors, Walker and Peter Firth are the driving force behind the growing romantic frisson between Ruth and Harry. 'The writers said that was rubbish and we were making it up, but we think there's long been something there.'

FIONA CARTER - OLGA SOSNOVSKA

Says Olga Sosnovska: 'I love playing ballsy women because I'm not ballsy at all. I'm really wet in real life.' Not as wet as all that. From a UK perspective, it is hard to imagine just how notorious Olga Sosnovska is in the USA, where – as Lena Kundera in *All My Children* – she had the first daytime TV lesbian kiss. Since then, she has become a lesbian icon and has campaigned for better acceptance and equality for gay men and women. Polish born, she is married to actor Sendhil Ramamurthy.

Series four had to be shot back to front because Sosnovska was about to have a baby. 'It was getting difficult to hide the growing bump behind a file all the time.' So the opening double-parter episodes one and two, in which she is off work 'recovering' from Danny's death and her near-miss, were shot right at the end of production. She now has a baby girl.

JO PORTMAN - MIRANDA RAISON

An aspiring young journalist, Jo first stumbled across the team when she got a visit from Adam dressed as a gas meter reader. Immediately suspicious, Jo's natural spying instincts prompted her to follow Adam to an MI5 safe house, where she got caught up in a shoot-out. Her quick thinking with the mobile phone – throwing it into the attacker's car as it auto-dialled her home answer phone – helped the team track down the perpetrators. Adam hires Jo from the crowd of over-qualified hopefuls, and the Grid gets a breath of new life.

Like series one actress Lisa Faulkner, Miranda Raison has done her own stint on TV soap *Holby City*. Her latest film is *Land of the Blind*, with Donald Sutherland and Ralph Fiennes.

ZAFAR YOUNIS - RAZA JAFFREY

Bright, funny and flirtatious, Zaf is quick-witted and can be a bit of a show-off – but he's always optimistic and full of good ideas. He can't stand whingers or slackers – and like Adam, never suffers fools gladly. Zaf's devious imagination makes him an asset in undercover work, although he can be impulsive and his threat analysis is weak. From a Muslim background, Zaf is not particularly devout – but is very sensitive to being patronised or misrepresented. He despises those who use their religion as an excuse for failure, or as a stick to beat society with.

Raza Jaffrey is the only star of *Spooks* to have come to fame via the traditional West End 'hoofing' route. A role as 'Sky' in the musical *Mamma Mia!* led on to the romantic lead in Andrew Lloyd Webber's *Bombay Dreams* and rave reviews for his performance as Akaash.

Trained at Bristol Old Vic Theatre school after a degree at Manchester University, he has also worked in television soaps such as *Casualty* and top-end theatre, playing Orsino in an all-Asian *Twelfth Night*.

JULIET SHAW – ANNA CHANCELLOR

A fast-burner in espionage's sooty skies, Juliet's Washington posting made for excellent contacts with the CIA. Perhaps a little too good: ex-lover Harry describes her as a ruthless right-wing crazy who'll stop at nothing. But Juliet's acid tongue and take-no-prisoners attitude is oddly attractive. Afraid of nobody, Juliet says the things that other people dare only think, like: 'How about we just kill him?'

Driven and single-minded, Juliet will tread on anybody who gets between her and what she wants – her own rapid climb to the top.

Anna Chancellor has made a career out of playing rich bitches and off-the-wall women in *Pride & Prejudice* and *Tipping the Velvet*. However, she is probably best known for her funny and memorable performance as 'Duckface' in the much-loved *Four Weddings and a Funeral*.

MALCOLM WYNN-JONES – HUGH SIMON

Unassuming to a fault, Malcolm is the backroom boy, often coming up with the vital piece of knowledge or equipment that turns an operation. Lonely, like Ruth, Malcolm is the old-fashioned English gentleman. Malcolm holds a bit of a candle for Zoe and sometimes, we suspect, for Ruth. A true chevalier, Malcolm may never break a lance or anyone's heart – but he can tell a terrible joke with winning panache.

Malcolm is a favourite with David Wolstencroft: 'It's like when you fall in love with somebody – it's just little things that get you. I love the way that Malcolm pretty much worshipped Zoe in this 'courtly love' way and would just every so often find ways to protect her or help...'

'Sometimes he can be gauche to the point of being a nerd,' says actor Hugh Simon. 'Sometimes, he can be almost witty and sophisticated. I think that the others can get quite irritated with him.' We suspect they are pretty fond of him, actually...

MANAGER My guests must not know...
MALCOLM They won't. No one sees us, we go through walls.
The MANAGER signs the official secrets act. TOM pockets it.
The MANAGER leaves.
TOM Just pop through the wall and get us a cup of tea would you Malcolm?
Grins all round. MALCOLM blushes.
MALCOLM Sorry, got a bit carried away there.

COLIN WELLS – RORY MACGREGOR

The technical wizard of the team, Colin will have your flat, your car and your undergarments bugged in the time it takes you to walk to the corner shop. A better pistol shot than Danny, thanks to his days on the biathlon trail, Colin will never have Danny's wit, style, or enthusiasm for designer gear; but he will always be the geek you learned to love. Peeping is Colin's business – and what he sees through those relentlessly unfashionable glasses doesn't bear thinking about – especially if you are Zoe. No security system is safe from him. No 'private' matter secure. Someone's always watching – and it's probably our Col.

Actor Rory MacGregor does not follow in Colin's techie footsteps, however. 'I'm not very computer literate, unfortunately. My computer crashes all the time and I have to ring people up and say: how do you do this?'

CHRISTINE DALE – MEGAN DODDS

Lovely Christine: witty, wry and sly; loyal to the Company, she is the CIA liaison officer whose cool duels with Tom are one of the pleasures of the show. But like Tom and Zoe, letting her feelings out of the bag gets Christine fed head-first into the espionage crusher. Slapped, falsely accused and disbelieved, in the end even this most brilliant of Uncle Sam's spooks goes the way of so many spies – down the chute into darkness, oblivion and series death.

Californian Megan Dodds now lives in London with her photographer husband. Possibly her most difficult role ever was the one-woman show at the Royal Court *My Name is Rachel Corrie*, in which Megan had to carry the show solo for one and a half hours. Like Olga, she is known for a lady kiss: in 2002 she was in *Up For Grabs*, a play in which she had to kiss Madonna.

TESSA PHILLIPS – JENNY AGUTTER

To a value-free, integrity-challenged risk-taker like Tessa Phillips, there's a vicious inner thrill to be had from betraying your country and your friends at the same time. Like many real spies who turn traitor, twenty-year Grid lifer Tessa does it both for the money and the inner satisfaction – otherwise known as overweening vanity – of believing she is smarter than the rest. Or maybe she's just bored. It takes only one slip, and man-eating Tessa makes it: claiming expenses for a string of phantom agents who exist only in the realms of her fertile imagination.

When Harry wants one of Tessa's invented *Spooks* to come good with some information, Zoe catches her out. But Tessa, showing anything but conscience, compounds the crime by offering shiny-bright Zoe £10,000 to keep stumm. Zoe turns her in, at which Harry gives Tessa the bin-liner/frogmarched out the door treatment double-quick. Gamekeeper turned poacher, a bitter enemy of MI5 is born. Machiavelli would be proud.

SAM BUXTON – SHAUNA MACDONALD

Hitting the Grid in the aftermath of a bomb attack, newly minted, fresh-out-of-training Sam Buxton's first job is – almost literally – to pick up the pieces. The least experienced person in the office, Sam is keen to prove that she can jump the *Spooks* bar. A little too keen, as the naïve, credulous side to her character makes her easy meat for the career manipulators lurking in the woodwork. Winding Sam up like a clockwork toy, Tessa uses her to undermine a serious anti-Colombian drugs cartel op. Leaving Sam, played by newcomer Shauna Macdonald, the willing fool forever floundering, career-nuked. Machiavelli would be in despair.

JOOLS SIVITER – HUGH LAURIE

Snake oil salesman isn't in it: MI6 head Siviter does cynical, sarcastic and supercilious like no one else, elevating condescension to an art form. Siviter's global scorn for sister service MI5 is most marked in his relentless dismissal of 'Little terrier Tom' – but then, Siviter doesn't really respect anyone or anything, not even himself. Routinely deceitful, often playing a double-game that runs directly against MI5's interests, Siviter often as not over-reaches himself, and needs the likes of Harry and Tom to pull his irons out of the fire.

The role of Siviter helped Hugh Laurie break out of the comedy mould in which he might otherwise have remained, and take international wing as the dishy but no less acerbic Dr Gregory House in hit US hospital drama *House*.

ROYAL OPERA HOUSE – NIGHT.
Tight on JOOLS SIVITER.
Straight to his face. His cheeks are stained with tears as Wotan sings his Act II monologue.
He takes a vibrating mobile out. He begins to text message. A WOMAN leans into view.
WOMAN *Do you mind awfully not doing that?*
JOOLS tight on his words.

JOOLS Are you a Nazi, madam?
WOMAN I beg your pardon?
JOOLS I mean, we Wagner fans are a pretty rum lot. I myself bugger skinheads, so kindly don't tell me what I can or cannot do.

Laurie is an ex-Dragon School boy, which for the uninitiated means one of those Englishmen brought up with 'must achieve' stamped on their forehead. His father was an Olympic gold rower, and Laurie himself rowed at Cambridge, where surprisingly, he got a third class degree – in Anthropology and Archaeology. He had suddenly discovered acting, and became President of the Footlights.

OLIVER MACE – TIM McINNERNY

Perfectly named for the role he plays in *Spooks*, Mace is a war hammer, clubbing away at MI5 and all its works. Epitomising the curled-lip bully it warms the cockles of your heart to hate, Mace is another incarnation of the enemy within – in his case, from the heart of the very Establishment our *Spooks* are trying to protect. Never expect thanks for helping anyone – especially if that someone is Oliver Mace. He'll only hate you for it – and despise you for doing a good job.

Writer Howard Brenton, who had worked with actor Tim McInnerny in the theatre and knew he could play a great villain, devised the role with him in mind. Like Hugh Laurie, Tim, who shot to fame as the upper-class twit in the hit series *Blackadder*, was in danger of remaining typecast and in comedy limbo. Not any more. Can this guy do serious? Can he ever.

AND FOR SERIES FIVE?...

Says screenwriter Ben Richards: 'For the new spook Ros Myers, played by Hermione Norris, I wrote the first three episodes and had a lot of input. She's an interesting character – they are not always going to be nice or make choices that we would necessarily make. And I felt that we needed someone who was a little more morally ambiguous. As Ros herself says, the whole point of a spy is that their morality is a pretty utilitarian one. It has to be, for the "greater good".'

EPISODE
GUIDE

SPOOKS 1.1

DIRECTOR: BHARAT NALLURI

[Scriptwriter: David Wolstencroft]

> *Global terrorism, Islamic extremists, all phone-tap resources plus Echelon pointed at the Middle East, and now the old enemy looks like it's rearing its ugly head...and it's such a beautiful morning...Harry Pearce*

The first time *Spooks* hit our television sets, a couple of things became instantly clear: first, we were on the end of some brilliant writing; and second, this streetwise, super-slick production was taking no prisoners. Viewers were going to have to work to keep up with what was happening, pay strict attention or else risk losing the plot.

The breakneck pace of the opening episode set the tone for the whole series, its sense of urgency and realism heightened by the post-9/11 mindset of intense fear. Episode 1.1 writer David Wolstencroft shows us there is no comfort zone. When it comes to international terrorism, Western counter-espionage agencies like MI5 are now dealing with a shadowy, elusive Hydra. Chop off one head, and the chances are that two more will grow in its place. The faceless enemy, who can strike anywhere, at any time and in any way is the one we all fear most. It's enough to make you paranoid.

Right from the off, a huge counterpoint is set up between the private and the personal. The very first time we meet Tom Quinn, he is in bed with his new lover. We don't know his name – but neither, it turns out, does the new love of his life, Ellie. As far as she knows, this handsome knight in shining armour is called Matthew ... and he works in IT.

By contrast, the first time we see beautiful, pensive Zoe, she is in bed by herself. Someone knocks at the door: it's her over-amorous landlord. She has a chair jamming the door handle. Immediately, you get the tension: living life as a spy is not easy. You only get three choices: live a lie; live alone; or live with a colleague, the officially approved solution.

Danny – aka 'Chris Patterson' has had a tip-off from a terrified informant, Osprey. Twenty explosive devices have been smuggled into Liverpool. Osprey doesn't know why, nor where they are going. Harry Pearce, MI5 head of counter-terrorism, assumes it's his 'old enemy' the IRA. But as always in *Spooks*, nothing is as it first seems. If you see a street cleaner dropping a bin bag in the road, you have to ask why – because cleaners don't drop litter. And as family planning doctor Karen Lynott gets into her car to go to work, we see she is being watched.

As she drives along the ordinary suburban street, American pro-life extremist Mary Kane detonates a bomb by text message. It's concealed in the bin bag.

We are left wondering what all this is about. A young mother is dead, her seven-year-old daughter dying. What can they have possibly done to deserve this? As we cut to a stuffy formal press tour of Thames House, M15's plush new HQ, Tom discovers two things. First that the Lynotts, both doctors, have been getting hate mail because of their pro-choice stance on abortion; second, that extremist Mary Kane (*right*), already sentenced to death because of a major bomb attack in her native Florida, has somehow sneaked past immigration into the UK. Her husband has been sentenced to execution: the team surmise she is aiming the next attack to time with his up-coming birthday.

Ice-slick, Tom has the team mount a large-scale surveillance operation to penetrate this new terrorist threat on its home turf. Zoe gets a surprise as they settle down for the night:

ZOE They'll be asleep.
SPODDY GUY This kit's so sensitive we should be able to hear them breathing.
He switches the kit on. We hear heavy breathing...and moaning.
ZOE looks at him. Creeping horror on her face.
The sound of sex. ZOE and the guy settle in awkwardly to listen – ZOE listens with professional detachment. SPODDY GUY, on the other hand, is loving it. ZOE finds this repulsive.
ZOE So much for a righteous woman. Enjoying yourself?
SPODDY GUY She is. You?

Meanwhile, new lover Tom is forced to meet Ellie's 'best friends' and see whose patience cracks first. Only Tom's covering is micro-thin. He has to bore for Britain all night to maintain his fictional persona – dull civil service IT specialist Matthew. And it is Ellie and little daughter Maisie who hold the balancing moral counter of this story. As she says to her friends: 'After Mark – I mean, when he left...and I found out I was pregnant, I'm ashamed to say I was in two minds...To think I even considered it!'

Tom, faced with nineteen bombs and a proven killer on the loose, sends Zoe undercover to pose as a sympathiser. The CIA are also on Mary Kane's trail, and are pushing to get her back in the USA, to face trial and probably Death Row. Tom can't afford to let Kane go until he's broken her UK network. Then the spooks strike gold: the surveillance team in the Wirral sift through Mary Kane's rubbish. Just under the cranberry juice, they find a pregnancy test. The only woman in that cottage is Mary. And she's positive.

They get a lead on the next target. Zoe poses as Dianne Sullivan, a gynaecologist and the intended victim. As Kane catches up with her in a crowded market, tension reaches breaking point as Danny tries to ensure that the bomb she's left near 'Dianne' in a holdall is jammed. But it's the MI5 jamming kit that's gone on the blink. Kane keys her mobile. Tom steps out of the surveillance van to arrest her...fifteen seconds left...ten, nine – the kit comes back on, blocking the trigger message with seconds to spare.

Is pro-life Mary going to want to lose her baby? Tom gets to work on her, pointing out that if MI5 hand her over to the CIA, the baby will die with her in the electric chair. She tells all, only to find that Tom, MI5 and the CIA don't make deals with terrorists.

Brave, in that it took a strong moral position on an ideological issue, the first episode had tested the audience with its sharpness, speed and style. More importantly, it exposed us to the murky MI5 world where truth is a variable concept. A world of confusing intelligence, disinformation, deals, counter-deals, broken promises and the ever-present threat of needless violence.

Karen Lynott's car after the bomb was detonated.

SPOOKS 1.2

DIRECTOR: BHARAT NALLURI

[Scriptwriter: David Wolstencroft]

'This time last year no one knew what a Muslim was. Now everyone's looking at people in the street. Where's he from, what's he doing...? Robert Osborne'

Episode 2 opens with the team attempting to bug the house of Robert Osborne, a known racist who is suspected of inciting riots across the country. He is also worryingly close to a mainstream politician, Bill Watson. MI5 attempts to monitor what's going on, but Osborne is so security-conscious – spectrum analysers, EM detectors, motion sensors – the mission has to be aborted. Not only that, one of the covert entry team has left a fuse on the floor, which might as well have been a big sign reading: 'You've been bugged.'

An internal team will have to go undercover. Meanwhile the experienced Zoe has been co-opted on an urgent Customs and Excise project, leaving Helen, a recent recruit, to go undercover with Tom.

They know from CCTV footage showing her black eye that Osborne is abusing his wife Claire (*overleaf, top*); in fact, we see her being forced to bare her breasts to his business colleagues and defend their young son from his volcanic temper. A weak point in the Osborne armour. Posing as IT teachers, Helen and Tom take over at Claire's weekly computing class. When they are invited to dinner, they find that Osborne is jealous and suspicious of any friends Claire makes. Alone with Osborne and highly nervous, Helen makes a huge mistake. Osborne trips her up with a simple test, asking casually: 'What does your boyfriend do again?' When she doesn't automatically pick him up – 'Steve's' her husband, not her boyfriend – she starts to gabble. And Helen has a vivid imagination...

HELEN He told you, didn't he?...Steve. Did he tell you? I was in the loo, I heard you two talking about something.
OSBORNE Yeah, I don't understand.
HELEN Our marriage...it's not what it seems. (*Osborne's listening now*) It's a bit more, um, it's a bit more relaxed. I...see other men. I don't really believe in monogamy. I don't think it's healthy for a long-term relationship...I didn't know if you knew, so...I'm sorry if I embarrassed you.

It's the worst thing she could have done. Osborne appears to accept her story, but slams the door in their face as they leave.

Meanwhile Zoe and Tessa, working on a human trafficking case, spot Osborne in some surveillance shots of the traffickers. What is he doing? 'Nick Thomas', an undercover journalist who is working with Osborne, reveals he is bringing asylum-seekers into the UK in their droves – forcing immigration into people's faces, and making it a problem that the government can't just ignore.

With their 'cover' rapidly peeling, Tom offers Claire £600 a week and a new identity if she will inform on her husband. The very next day Osborne sends his goons to abduct Tom and Helen. They've been playing with fire – Osborne is far more ruthless and efficient than they have realised. Already 'Nick' has been executed.

The next few minutes are some of the most terrifying ever seen on British television (*left*). To find out who Tom – already severely beaten – really is, Osborne puts first Helen's hand and then her head into a deep-fat fryer.

How does Tom escape? After the screaming adrenaline of the last few scenes, hardly anyone will remember. Nine million nauseous viewers almost certainly had their heads in their hands. It is Claire who, after Helen is shot, throws her lit cigarette into the fat fryer. In the huge explosion that follows, Tom runs headlong through a plate glass window.

Gorgeous Lisa Faulkner was the tabloids' darling. A former star of *Casualty*, *Brookside* and *Holby City*, the violent death of her charming character Helen Flynn – in only episode 2 – showed that *Spooks* was not going to play by other shows' rules.

Says Kudos' Stephen Garrett: 'We set Lisa up to be a regular member of the cast. She was probably the most famous cast member we had at the time, at least as far as the tabloids were concerned. Because she died, so horribly, it created an amazing tension for all the following episodes...

'No – this is not soap! They won't be "back next week".'

THE INCREMENT

Who are the strange, black-suited figures that Tom and Harry can call in at a moment's notice? Working across M15 and M16, 'The Increment' is drawn from elements of UK Special Forces: the SAS and the SBS. Based mainly at the Duke of York's barracks, they are on standby twenty-four hours a day. A small flight of helicopters – including a couple of Chinooks, with their dedicated Special Forces pilots – is always at their disposal. Not to mention an armoury of weapons for every occasion, drawn from across the globe.

Equipment? Souped-up, armoured Range Rovers that come with all the bells and whistles: burst-transmission, encoded satlink comms equipment; state-of-the-art anti-jamming frequency-hopping radios; specialist scaling ladders; moving map GPS; onboard Internet access for fast download of key info like building plans, internal layout of foreign embassies; weapons storage; anti-burst tyres. Increment personnel include parachute insertion specialists, experts in explosive entry, covert entry, bugging – the whole shebang. They bring top skills as world-class marksmen and ultra-fast drivers. And let's not forget a readiness to kill in the interests of the British state.

We asked former Increment members about episode 1.2, in which Robert Osborne murders a young MI5 officer in a most horrible way. Our contacts said they'd get a phone call: 'Fancy a drive in the country?' – code for an assassination job. Osborne might have an 'accident' that could be suicide – like a fall from a high cliff. But 'accidents' – especially car crashes – risk involving innocent third parties. The guys say it is much better if someone just 'disappears'.

SPOOKS 1.3

DIRECTOR: ROB BAILEY

[Scriptwriter: Simon Mirren]

> You created me. You trained me, manipulated me, just like the West manipulates entire countries, and then acts so shocked when they turn round and rip off the hand that fed them. **Johnny Marks**

A siege at the Turkish consulate. Kurds are demanding prisoner release in exchange for hostages, with Zoe stuck in the middle. The storyline, and even more so the images, are a strong reminder of the real-life 1980 Iranian Embassy siege.

Tom is jogging along the Grand Union Canal in Maida Vale. One of his 'snouts' has wind of some ex-Army types trying to buy small arms. Tom isn't interested – it's his 'family day', his birthday, and he's all set to spend it with Ellie and Maisie. But even after only two episodes, you know the job's going to get in the way ...

Tasked with conducting an annual check on MI5 listening devices planted inside the Turkish consulate, Zoe, posing as PR consultant Emily Arlington, has wangled an invitation to a consular reception.

For Zoe, it's a routine op – until, that is, a group of Kurdish freedom fighters led by Leyla Bakuri, a drop-dead gorgeous fanatical killer female, decide to spoil the party. They demand the release of fellow paramilitaries. To make things worse, they have the help of four ex-Special Forces Brits, one of whom, Johnny Marks [Christopher Fulford], looks mad, bad and very, very dangerous to know.

During a quick exchange between Marks and one of his former SF buddies we see a young female hostage, Tara Welks, tied up in the back of a taxi.

The dreaded flash message hits Tom's mobile. He still hasn't told Ellie his real job or even his real name, and now misses his own birthday party. Already in danger, Zoe is in for special terrorist treatment if the hostage-takers find her secret kit, including a lock-pick and videophone linked to the Grid.

The hostage-takers wire the Turkish consul – who is asthmatic – up to a bomb, lash him to a chair and stick him outside on the balcony. Despite the lovely view, he does not look at all happy. Colin and Danny get busy inserting a through-the-wall fibre-optic probe: it's essential MI5 knows what's going on in there.

Tara, now tied up in a dank basement, turns out to be the daughter of Cranborne Bank director Roger Welks. Cranborne is not just any old bank. Both MI5 and MI6 use it to pay their field agents. Worse, Roger has given Marks the 'swiftcodes', which unlock the agent accounts. Marks can now access the Security Service's millions, transfer a cool £15m to himself, find out the undercover identities of some 3,000 agents working for MI5 and MI6 and sell these details on to the highest bidder. If he succeeds, then Harry, his team and Britain's security services are finished.

From the grainy consular CCTV footage, Tessa recognises the terrorist taxi driver as ex-British SF/ex-convict Marks. Harry knows all about Marks – he is a serial traitor who betrayed the Brits, the Arabs and the IRA. But Harry is convinced that the Republicans killed Marks with a car bomb fifteen years ago – not least because he personally identified the remains. Tessa argues not – Marks is still very much alive. And she should know. She confesses to Harry she was in love with him.

Matters come to a head in the consulate when a terrorist finds Zoe's bag with its compromising kit inside. Leyla threatens to kill Steve, the Met policeman they are holding, unless the bag's owner comes forward. Zoe has to own up to being a spook – but maintains the 'Emily Arlington' cover. Tom and Harry action the SAS counter-terrorism team that will hit the hostage-takers if necessary (*right, top*). Marks starts transferring the millions to his own account. And begins downloading MI5 and MI6 agent details to a disk.

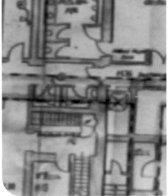

The team get a lucky break when Tessa finds a network of secret tunnels under the consulate (*right, bottom*). Colin fakes prisoner release pictures and gets them broadcast on TV news. The hostage-takers will be fooled into believing their demands have been met.

The Turkish consul starts to have the asthma attack he has been threatening throughout. Tom goes in hard with the Becotide puffer – and in a natty armoured vest.

True to past form, Marks now betrays and abandons the Kurds. He has the disk with the agent names. In pulling Zoe to safety, Tom gets shot, a flesh wound. The SO19 [Met police firearms branch] sniper covering him shoots one of the hostage-takers using a red laser sight. [This is known in British Special Forces as 'giving them the good news'.] With Danny's help, the SAS storm the building, arrest the terrorists and save the hostages. Danny – with a headlock – puts the squeeze on Marks's buddy to say where Marks has gone, but the man doesn't know. In the meantime Tara is found safe and well in the flat Marks has rented.

Tessa goes home to find Marks waiting in her beautiful flat. Before his faked death, Tessa handled field agent Johnny Marks only too well: he made her pregnant, but the baby – a girl – terminated naturally. He is shocked when Tessa tells him.

Tom limps off home to tell Ellie the truth about Tom Quinn – maybe. Harry turns up with the boys to arrest Marks outside Tessa's. Harry assumes Marks has the agent list hidden somewhere, and Marks lets him think so. In fact, Tessa has it on her coffee table – which leaves us wondering: has he simply forgotten it, or are he and Tessa doing a deal? The question isn't answered.

Harry tells Marks he does his own dirty work – assassinations – if he has to. And in so doing admits he killed Marks's brother. The spooks have saved the day – but a vengeful former 'asset' has come very, very close to inflicting terminal damage on Britain's security services.

The striking Sufi music used in this episode is called 'Anadolu Giftellisi'. Sufi is a secret Turkish religious sect.

Tom takes a birthday bullet.

SPOOKS 1.4

DIRECTOR: ROB BAILEY

[Scriptwriter: Howard Brenton]

> ' You can't pull Peter Salter – he's a legend! Danny Hunter '

What is loyalty? And loyalty to whom? Episode 1.4 really turns the screw on Tom and Zoe's idealism as, surrounded by cynicism, dishonesty and distrust, they attempt to work out right from wrong, honesty from *realpolitik*. Wounded during the siege on the State Consulate of Turkey, Tom is under constant pressure from girlfriend Ellie to tell her the truth about his double life. Meanwhile, Danny and Zoe have recognised a top MI5 agent, Peter Salter, taking part in an anti-globalisation rally. Salter is on a deep cover joint MI5/MI6 infiltration op to catch Istvan Vogel, an extreme anarchist with, the team suspects, ambitions to disrupt President Bush's upcoming visit to the UK. Terminally.

Charming, urbane Salter is an Oxford 'Blue' and confirmed quoter of Shakespeare. His spying record and success with women are legendary. While Danny and Zoe worry that they are in trouble for blowing his cover, Salter runs the sister services a merry dance. Has he fallen in love with super-gorgeous society drop-out Andrea, his link to the anarchists? Or is he playing some deep game all of his own? Salter doesn't know he's being bugged during this exchange:

ANDREA I trusted you. I told myself I was in love with you.
PETER You've got to believe me. I'm the thing a security service fears the most. The spy who goes through traitor's gate, willingly…and embraces everything he's been trained to destroy. (*Throaty now.*) I want to be with you. I want to be one of you. I've learnt from you. There is a world elsewhere.'

Watching the surveillance footage from the backroom of a newspaper shop, Tom, Harry and dreadful MI6 chief Jools Siviter are mesmerised. Typically, it's the arch-cynic Siviter who breaks the silence: 'Is that a quote from something?' It's Shakespeare's *Coriolanus*. Tom, who was recruited and trained by Salter and is, after all, lovestruck himself, has a gut instinct that Peter has 'turned'. He pulls him from the mission, but allows him one last meeting – undisturbed – with Andrea.

Like the practised agent he is, Salter gets rid of his tail – Danny and Zoe – by ringing the police and claiming they are making love in the car. He and Andrea meet up with Vogel and get clean away.

Harry, keen to get back on top of the case, asks Tessa to activate one of her covert agents – working undercover with a related anarchist group. He insists that it's Zoe who must meet and brief the agent. As Salter prepares to break into a university campus and hack into its computers, Zoe discovers that Tessa's 'agent' does not exist. Tessa has been running a series of phantom (non-existent) agents and pocketing the money. She offers Zoe £10,000 to keep quiet.

A furious Harry discovers Danny has been using his spy skills to fiddle his own credit rating and makes him cut up his credit card. He is sent to do training as punishment.

Salter is arrested and dragged back to HQ (*left*). It's impossible to tell for sure whether Salter is a traitor or not. He gives Tom some good, real information – he recognised their secret training ground as the old Cernwyth army range, north of the Black Mountains: 'Cheeky though, eh? Terrorists holing up on a derelict MoD site.' Yet he is adamant that he can't live without Andrea. Unable to live the life of a double-agent any longer, he hangs himself.

While the management put on a show of having infiltrated Vogel's network and stopped him doing anything more serious than break into a university, Danny's quick wits redeem him. There's one question niggling in his mind. Why would super-agent Salter bother to infiltrate a university geography department? It suddenly hits him – Salter has used the department's computers to hack in to Air Traffic Control and alter critical flight information. The President's plane is diverted to Paris. Phew!

TO BE, OR NOT TO BE?
Anthony Head, former cult regular on *Buffy the Vampire Slayer* and one of the UK's most popular actors, plays the suave but suffering Peter Salter.

'I read this and thought: "This is a phenomenal script." Then I turned back to the front page and it said: "Written by Howard Brenton." Wow! I worked with Howard at the National Theatre: you know TV is moving in the right direction when you see someone like him writing for it.'

So what is the actual line Salter quotes to romance the gorgeous Andrea (Bronwen Davies)? Brenton reveals that he mis-quoted Shakespeare's great war anti-hero Coriolanus: 'There is a world elsewhere...' The playwright has a penchant for anti-heroes. Postmodern to the last, tortured hero Salter quotes both T.S. Eliot and Shakespeare's *Hamlet* as he smashes up the hidden camera he knows MI6 has trained on him: 'Good night sweet ladies, good night.'

SPOOKS 1.5

DIRECTOR: ANDY WILSON

[Scriptwriter: Howard Brenton]

❛ It's a good outcome all round, Harry. A nasty "foreign" is dead; a dodgy Brit disgraced. **Jools Siviter** ❜

❛ Ship afloat. **Harry Pearce** ❜

A pitch-black night in the desert; automatic weapons blazing. Two beaming Westerners, incongruous in flowing Arab dress, discuss the generosity of their host, Sheikh Rasul. Champagne flows.

Fast forward ten years: we meet one of those men, Hampton Wilder, once again. Only this time, he is leaving the gates of Her Majesty's Prison, Edgefield. As the press surge to interview the former minister, Wilder declares he wants to apologise. 'The pleasures of life overwhelmed me. I abused the sacred trust of my high office. I lied, I stole public money, and I have now paid for that mistake.'

In a delightfully tongue-in-cheek reference to the case of Christian convert and former Conservative minister Jonathan Aitken, Wilder then declares: 'I now go into private life. The one shining thing for me, from my time in prison, is to have found that the Lord Jesus is my saviour.'

Danny pulls Wilder into a waiting car. Wilder has asked to meet with Harry 'this had better be about something big' Pearce at MI5. The meeting with the team takes place in the Thames House underground car park in full dinner dress. Self-ironising Harry has just been on a seminar about disorientation techniques...But Wilder gets the upper hand when he asks them to join him in prayer.

It is something big. Wilder has written his memoirs, and they implicate parliamentary star and Prime Ministerial crony Richard Maynard in some very dodgy arms dealing. He claims Maynard is working hand in hand with Sheikh Rasul's Mr Fixit – a Russian by the name of Sergei Lermov. The memoirs have been stolen...and Downing Street doesn't want them hitting the shelves.

Tessa is adamant they are being sold a line. Harry calls in Maynard, ostensibly to brief him about gun-runner Lermov's threat to national security – and to ask the government to carry out an audit of weapons stocks. Maynard's cool does not crack. Pretending not to know Maynard personally, Tessa leads the politician to a 'dead spot' in Thames House ['...a bonk in the MI5 building, that's got to be worth some air miles'].

When Tom tracks Lermov down, he seems to co-operate, if

reluctantly. He confirms that Maynard is corrupt. Yet, as Harry says, 'MI5 doesn't "do" evil – just treachery, treason and Armageddon.' Someone is lying here, but is it necessarily Maynard? Tom gets the impression that Lermov is being protected . . .

Zoe and Danny, meanwhile, have been playing 'the Game': spying on each other. Danny gets home to find Zoe drunk on his hidden vodka. The secret she carries about Tessa's phantom agents is weighing her down. 'She gave me money,' she blurts. 'You mean the ten grand next door,' he says coolly, 'behind the plug socket?'

When Lermov is suddenly murdered, Harry and Tom pull MI6 head Jools Siviter out of a Wagner concert. Siviter, as ever, has outflanked them. Not only was Lermov his agent, but the SIS boss already has Wilder's memoirs.

The memoirs are leaked, Siviter pinning it on MI5, and Maynard is forced to resign. Harry is furious and the two agency heads joust, drink for drink, in Siviter's club. Siviter finally admits that he wanted to discredit Maynard for very good reasons – he looked set to become Foreign Secretary. Only problem being, he's a long-term CIA asset . . .

The trouble for Tom, Zoe and Danny is that they don't, as Jools Siviter says, 'do ambiguity'. Danny has convinced Zoe she must 'burn', i.e. expose, Tessa. What she doesn't know is that Tessa is a lot more dangerous than she seems: to protect her old flame Maynard, she's the one who had Lermov killed.

As Siviter says: 'Thank God someone's running the country while the rest of us are at the opera.'

HARRY Was it worth it?
JOOLS You're not a Wagner fan, are you . . .
HARRY Isn't it the most repugnant music ever written?
JOOLS (*Not at all put out.*) It is a bit of a closet thing these days. People can't handle the dark side.

SPOOKS 1.6

DIRECTOR: ANDY WILSON

[Scriptwriter: Howard Brenton/David Wolstencroft]

❛ If they do what I think they're gonna do, most of Ireland's uninhabitable for the next two hundred years. Not to mention everything north of Bristol. Patrick McCann ❜

A man walks into a safe house with a grenade in his pocket. He is Patrick McCann, section commander in a splinter IRA group, personally responsible for the torture and murder of at least twenty RUC policemen and two MI5 officers. And he has some information.

Harry is more than usually testy. Tessa has gone way over her remit in admitting the Irishman into the safe house. 'You've called the cavalry, I take it?' 'He said Asabiyah, Harry ... Asabiyah,' she replies. 'This isn't about Ireland.'

Harry is adamant. There will be no deals with McCann. He would like to go further, and 'bring about a curtailment of his continuing existence through proxy' ... kill him. But the team is worried – an ultra-extremist terrorist cell with links to Al-Qaeda, Asabiyah has so far been impenetrable. If McCann is ready to risk so much by storming an MI5 safe house alone, this must be important.

Tom meets McCann in the middle of a field (*right*). The two men stop about twenty feet away from each other and strip, to prove they're not wearing wires. 'Davy Crockett, I presume,' jokes McCann. 'Anyone seeing this would think we're in some fecky farmer's porn video.'

The news is bad. McCann's group has been 'freelancing' – training Asabiyah – and came across a very detailed schematic of Sefton B nuclear power station. McCann, who wants to protect Ireland from the fallout, promises names, routes, dates and access – if Tom will agree to 'keep a blind eye' to his own group till sunrise Thursday.

Harry is appalled. The team want to agree to the deal. Harry pulls rank – and says no. So Tom goes over Harry's head to the Director-General.

An incandescent Harry finds out that GCHQ has just picked up a Pay As You Go mobile keyword. An Irish splinter group plans to hit Broadstreet railway station at rush hour the next morning. Admitting he is over-emotional, he explains that McCann murdered his best friend. He still insists that McCann can't be trusted to honour any deal, and that the real threat to Broadstreet must take precedence over the 'fictional' threat to Sefton B. Just to make Harry's day, Zoe finally cracks, and tells him about Tessa's treachery. Tessa is escorted from the building.

Tom takes Danny and Zoe aside – they are going to run a fake operation to fool Harry. Tom's view is that the bomb should go ahead – but 'accidentally on purpose, this thing hurts no one. It can be done.'

Tom, who has just had elaborate security fitted to his house to lure Ellie back into his life, has underestimated the danger he is in. The cover-up at Broadstreet is a qualified success, and McCann gives Tom a laptop with information about the Sefton B raid. Zoe and Danny have already done the reconnaissance work. McCann's information helps Danny work out the three optimum angles of fire. Two 'ramblers' with a LAW 90 anti-tank weapon are quietly shot. Danny is jubilant. 'Correct me if I'm wrong, but did we just stop half the country from being nuked?'

Weary from being dragged around and beaten by McCann's heavies, Tom goes home with the laptop. He carefully stores it in a filing cabinet drawer: puts the key in another box and locks that.

But Maisie accidentally locks Tom out of the house, and the new security precautions mean he can't get back in. Almost simultaneously, he gets a warning call from McCann: his colleagues have rigged Tom's laptop, thinking it would go back to MI5. It has six ounces of C4 explosive in it – enough to blow up the house.

The series ends with a massive cliffhanger. Will Ellie and Maisie die? Will Tom, as he hangs on for grim life by the letterbox (*left*)?

An explosion rips across the screen ...

SPOOKS 2.1

DIRECTOR: BHARAT NALLURI

[Scriptwriter: Howard Brenton]

DANNY Tom, the sky is falling.
TOM My family need me right now.
DANNY This is from the top. There's no negotiation on this, mate.
I'm sorry.

In a bit of a hole with this one, writer Howard Brenton had to keep Tom's girlfriend Ellie and her daughter Maisie alive. We all thought they'd been killed by a laptop bomb Tom thoughtlessly took home at the conclusion to series one.

It was a plant – of course. Meant to distract MI5 from the real target, the bomb in Tom's house failed to detonate. The IRA bomb we actually saw explode killed the terrorists' true objective, Secretary of State for Northern Ireland Michael Purefoy.

Tom's contact Davy McCann, a member of the IRA splinter cell that planted both devices, offers to defect and work for MI5. But MI5 loses the race to pick McCann up. Shot dead, the label tied to his toe reads: 'Property of MI5'.

New recruit Sam Buxton arrives to find the Grid in meltdown. Harry is getting it in the neck for failing to protect a crucial member of the government. And a mortar attack has just hit Longcross military base. Is this second attack a new IRA campaign? And who would know about this top-secret base? Harry suspects a leak from somewhere deep in the heart of the MoD.

Forced to work, Tom brings Ellie and Maisie with him into Thames House – where Ellie proves characteristically ungrateful: 'This isn't for me – it's for you.'

Forged passports alert the team to the UK arrival of Miloslav Gradic, a wanted Serb war criminal 'with a taste for genocide' who has been on the run for six years. A NATO bombing raid during the Bosnian war killed both his sons, and Gradic is out for revenge.

Watching a news report on the Purefoy bombing, Ellie decides she's had enough of risking her own and her daughter's safety. When Tom comes to find them, they're gone.

Back in harness, Tom tasks Zoe to check out known Gradic sympathiser 'Rado', a cipher clerk at the Serbian embassy. Tom is in for a sleepless night: Ellie and Maisie have left him. No messages. Spotted by old school friend Sarah on the way home, Zoe has to avoid her by

hiding in an alleyway. But things improve when Carlo, a dishy Italian, starts chatting up Zoe in the pub. Jealous, Danny teases Zoe when she fails to follow up:

DANNY Erm, so what put you off exactly? His looks? His charm? His money? Too single, was he?
ZOE Every once in a while...you know...it just gets to me. (*Beat*) Look at Tom and Ellie. They were perfect for each other. And the job's made mincemeat out of them. If they can't make it, what chance do the rest of us have? (*Beat*) What chance have I got?

It's a feeling that Tom expresses even more forcefully:

TOM One minute they're just innocent, they're safe. Then you open your mouth. A few words come out. 'I'm a spy.' And suddenly they're a target, a liability for life, and it's all your fault. You've branded them. It's like a hex.

Convinced Gradic has the weaponry stolen in the Longcross attack, the spooks target Rado as a way of getting to him. Exploiting Rado's interest in films, Zoe goes undercover in a video store custom-made by MI5.

Faking a road traffic accident, Gradic's men shoot an army munitions convoy to pieces (*left*). It must be an inside job. Danny starts trawling the bank accounts of junior MoD personnel.

Back at the shop, Zoe almost blows it by pushing Rado too hard, too soon. Then pesky school friend Sarah reappears, threatening disaster. Thinking on her feet, Zoe ducks behind a partition and convinces Rado that Sarah is a jealous rival. At first suspicious, Rado offers to help 'Kate' find a better job by rewriting her CV. Which will now act as a control document for the bugged cufflinks Zoe gives Rado, allowing Colin to read the keystrokes on Rado's embassy computer.

Back on the Grid, Malcolm finds out that Rado is not just Gradic's nephew, but a fellow killer: Zoe is in much more danger than they thought. Tasked to keep an eye on her, Danny gets himself mugged and injured outside Rado's flat. Attractive Accident & Emergency doctor Vicky Westbrook hits on the visiting Tom hard: 'Well, there *is* a God.' Ignoring this, Tom begs for – and gets – a meeting with Ellie and Maisie.

Deciphering Rado's keystrokes, Colin and the spooks realise he is communicating with Gradic through the *Evening Standard*'s small ads [*pace* John Buchan's *The Thirty-nine Steps*]. Danny finds the source of the MoD leak – junior official Jim North. Under interrogation North explains the basic code he and the Serbs used. Scouring the pages of the *Evening Standard*, Malcolm decodes the key message – the next attack is on COBRA – the top-level Cabinet/Defence/Intelligence committee the Prime Minister has convened to discuss the recent spate of attacks. With only a few minutes left to prevent the attack, a frantic Tom gets a new mobile phone ultimatum from Ellie:

ELLIE The job or us, Tom...I am well past upset. Maisie and I love you, Tom, and we need you to choose. Now, please.
TOM I can't do that this second.
ELLIE Then you've made your choice. Sorry.

With Gradic's gang apparently poised to strike, the story wrong-foots us: Harry has moved the COBRA meeting to a different venue, leaving Tom and Special Forces to arrest Gradic in a counter-ambush at the original site. Near breaking point, Tom orders a Special Forces soldier to hand him his weapon so that he can shoot Gradic dead. Luckily, the soldier refuses to obey.

Gradic will escape any real justice. But Tom has an idea: why not make Gradic the subject of 'extraordinary rendition'? Send him to Egypt with a 'paedophile' label tied round his neck? 'You know what the Egyptians do to sex offenders?' Rado, too, is arrested.

Rebuffed by Ellie when he tries to see Maisie, Tom gives up. There's only so much humiliation a chap can take. Even when – especially when – he's in love.

SPOOKS 2.2

DIRECTOR: BHARAT NALLURI

[Scriptwriter: Howard Brenton]

' Shall I tell you a secret? One day England will become the house of Islam. No hamburgers, no cans of lager. All of the people of this island will honour God and follow His prophet, peace be upon Him...Mohammed Rachid '

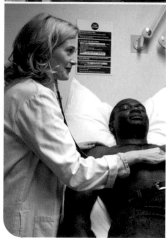

Visceral and shocking, this episode by Howard Brenton was screened only three weeks after Al-Qaeda attacks in Casablanca and Riyadh. The month before, the far-right British National Party won eight council seats in Burnley; four months before that, Abu Hamza al-Masri was banned from preaching at the Finsbury Park mosque in London for openly praising Osama Bin Laden and the attacks on the Twin Towers.

It's dark. Inside a surveillance van at night. The atmosphere is tense: Tom barks at Danny. How long has it been since the wire went down?

Too long. Johnny, the too-young double-agent Tom has sent into the Birmingham Parkmount mosque is blown. Extremist cleric Mohammed Rachid is interrogating him, the tell-tale wire in his hand. In the bare-boarded, strip-lit room a group of young men surround the panic-stricken Johnny. Moderate, displaced mosque leader Fazul Azzam tries to intervene, then leaves. Rachid's men bind Johnny's feet. And start to cane them.

In the obbo van, a heated argument. Danny wants back-up. Tom is thinking big picture. 'We can't have special forces barging into a mosque, Danny.' Just as they decide to go in 'and ask for their friend back' a large object smashes onto the van: Johnny.

In hospital, just before the brain haemorrhage that turns him into a cabbage, Johnny tells Tom about Rachid's 'nest of angels', a team of boy suicide bombers. At the time when he is most needed, MI5 has let down and lost one of its few effective Muslim agents.

Enter Ibhn Khaldun, illegally and via the Channel Tunnel. A stick in one hand, exhausted but pushing determinedly through the crowds, he looks every inch the 'Old Testament prophet in the rush hour' of Brenton's imagination.

'Her name's Vicky Westbrook,' Danny tells Tom. She's the Doc who patched him up when he was mugged in 2.1. Tom affects nonchalance: 'Did I notice her?'

'She noticed you...Sorry don't mind me saying this do you, after Ellie...But you've got to ride the bicycle again, Boss.'

Posing as an immigration official, Tom informs Rachid his citizenship application will fail. Grooming sixteen-year-old Abu Hassan as a suicide bomber, Rachid is unfazed. 'What a bad apology for an intelligence service.'

At this low point, Ruth Evershed arrives on the Grid. On loan from GCHQ, her encyclopedic knowledge, lateral thinking and trap-like memory immediately change the game. Hacking into the French Security Service she discovers that Scotland Yard has unwisely turned down Khaldun's offer to spy for the UK.

RUTH
'Oh you're in here. Oh sorry!' This is when we first meet Ruth Evershed. Brenton describes her thus: 'She enters with files and books spilling from her arms, some landing on the table, some on the floor. Mid-thirties, she has disastrous fashion sense, but it is at least all hers. Everything about her says "very self-conscious" and "very, very bright".' She joins from GCHQ, to run intelligence analysis. With her, she brings a new approach, and an entirely different kind of mind:

Khaldun reveals that Rachid is linked to the GAJ – the Group of Algerian Jihad – which is financing extremist groups in Britain. Tom and Harry have serious worries that they may be taking on a dangerous double-agent, but recruit Khaldun to infiltrate the Parkmount mosque.

While Zoe hangs around hoping to meet handsome banker Carlo again, Tom has Doctor Vicky and CIA liaison Christine Dale circling him. Taking the plunge, he sleeps with sexy Vicky [Natasha Little]:

TOM There was a woman and a child that I let down...
VICKY No don't tell me. I'd rather think of you as weird than boring tragic, OK?
TOM OK.

But running Khaldun means Tom can't stay in London: instead of being with his new lover, it's off to read the *Koran* in a bedsit.

In the mosque, Khaldun plays a dangerous game of double-bluff. When Rachid asks how an illegal immigrant got a job in the University, Khaldun replies: 'The job was arranged for me by the British Intelligence Services. My instructions by our brothers were to infiltrate British Security. It was, praise to God, disarmingly easy to do so.'

Is Khaldun a double-agent? He misses three of his contact meetings with Tom and then turns up in the middle of the night. The news is bad: there will be an attack the next day, using the boy. Khaldun is meant to take Abu Hassan into Birmingham city centre, and intends trying to talk him out of it. With the risk of mass death and injury, Tom can't sanction that. Khaldun ends the disagreement by knocking Tom out.

Faced with disaster, MI5 raids the mosque and arrests Rachid. They find suicide bombers' vests, but can't force the boy's location from Rachid. With the clock ticking, they approach Fazul Azzam, whose daughter has been spying for Rachid. In a moment of real dramatic irony, wise man of peace Azzam shuts the door and beats the information out of the girl.

The climax comes in a children's playground (*below*). Hard on Hassan's heels, Tom and Special Forces clear the area. Fighting his way past two of Rachid's henchmen to get to Hassan, Khaldun shows huge courage in trying to persuade the boy to give up. But when Hassan pulls the detonator cord, they both die.

RUTH (*following a briefing on the mosque*) Sounds like some jolly trade-craft. How did they know you were in the obbo van?'
ZOE No idea.
RUTH Ah. Ramallah whispers.
ZOE I'm sorry...?
RUTH The Palestinians are terrific at it. People at windows, on street corners...They signal each other where an enemy vehicle's passing.

SPOOKS 2.3

DIRECTOR: ROB BAILEY

[Scriptwriter: Matthew Graham]

> Know what scares me? That one day I'll get a bump on the head and all these people I have to be are all going to get fused together in my psyche. I'll be one helluva schizophrenic. **Zoe Reynolds**

Pistol-packing Danny and team evacuate a Stoke Newington school because of a supposed asbestos problem. In fact, MI5 has tracked the source of a hack on its own mainframe computer to this school. Chief suspect is schoolteacher and ex-Socialist Freedom Movement [SFM] activist Gordon Blakeney.

Danny finds the rogue computer and pulls the plug – but the spider counting down on its screen makes him think it's booby-trapped. Instead of exploding, it emits a shriek. The serious damage: the hack wipes 'Antony and Cleopatra', two undercover agents investigating arms trafficking in western Pakistan, off the GPS map. Communication is impossible, leaving the assets stranded.

Harry plays it all down: 'Someone just put their hand up our skirt.' But bookworm Ruth explains the hacker's gnomic classical message:

ZOE (*reads from screen*) 'Zeus spoke and nodded with his darkish brows and immortal locks fell forward from the lord's deathless head, and he made great Olympus tremble.'
RUTH *The Iliad*. Homer. Eighth century BC. The quote's a threat. Olympus was the seat of power in ancient Greece. Here, it trembles. So, whoever they are, they want to bring us down.
HARRY A little inflammatory, Ruth.

Ruth is right. But Harry wants still-not-yet-trusted Ruth out of the loop.

Posing as a freelance journalist – something the real MI5 tries very hard not to do – Danny infiltrates SFM's *Red Cry* newspaper. As for Blakeney, '…we have a vicious anarchist who just happens to be handing out pamphlets yards from a computer that's hacking into MI5. We bug his work, his home, his entire life.'

Tom sends Zoe in undercover as English teacher Jane Graham. Danny, meanwhile, offers *Red Cry* editor James Crow a massive scoop – MI5 raided the school, not council asbestos monitors. Danny claims

he has a Home Office mole, and that he cares more about the socialist cause than kudos.

Tom tells new girlfriend Vicky right up-front that he works for MI5. Her teasing is hugely refreshing after ultra-needy Ellie.

TOM I can tell you, because they've checked you and you're clean.
VICKY They clearly haven't seen me after a thirty-six-hour shift.

Forced to take the second hack attack on MI5's mainframe seriously, Harry states the threat: 'If these sods find a way to hack into the Inner Sanctum then every operative will suffer the same fate as Antony and Cleopatra. MI5 will be powerless – as will this country.' There's massive pressure on Zoe to get something on Blakeney – fast.

Faced with a classroom of adolescents, Zoe is trying to teach without any kind of experience or training (*left*). A watching Tom comments wryly: 'Give me an Afghan drugs deal any day.' Ever loyal, Malcolm thinks she's 'splendid'. Careful and suspicious, Blakeney turns down Zoe's offer of a drink and heads off to the IT room – the only classroom the spooks have not obboed up. Reminding Zoe she is not a real teacher, Tom suggests she wear her tight blue sweater. Guaranteed to get Blakeney's attention. And that of about seven million viewers.

Zoe spots Blakeney leaving school and goes after him. But Blakeney is only trying to help Peter, one of his pupils, who has been bullied. Peter says his Dad will sort it out.

It can be difficult dealing with people who are paranoid for a living, and left-wing journalists are a breed unto their own. The SFM guys suspect Danny's ear stud is a listening device. This time they are right: Danny is blown.

Arriving at *Red Cry* as MI5 rounds up the usual suspects, Blakeney runs into Zoe and her 9mm pistol. Under interrogation, the teacher protests SFM and *Red Cry*'s innocence: 'You're not only barking up the wrong tree, you're in the wrong flaming forest.'

The twist in the tale is that 'bullied' Peter is the real – and very brilliant – hacker, acting, we are led to believe, on his father's orders. Peter hacks into MI5's mainframe again, this time leaving the clue '94' – Plutonium on the periodic table.

Panicking, Tom and Zoe get readings that suggest the school is a 'radioactive hot zone'. They evacuate both the school and MI5's 'roadworks hut' forward control point outside, which gives Peter the opportunity he's engineered: the chance to hack directly into MI5's computer system via Malcolm's abandoned laptop and start downloading files.

Finding the Geiger scrambler that has been generating the false radiation readings, Tom accuses Blakeney of planting it. Zoe points out he was in the forward control shed. 'Not alone,' Blakeney counters.

Making Blakeney's connection to Peter, Zoe catches him red-handed hacking into MI5's mainframe. At this critical moment, stranded agent 'Cleopatra' sends a new appeal for help: her partner, Antony, is dead. Can they help her get out? Ruth breaks the coded Titan/Zeus message – like the myth, it's a reference to a powerful child. But without their computer network, the spooks are powerless. Peter's real name – Noah Gleeson – rings a bell: this is the son of Victor Gleeson, MI5's former man in Athens. Working undercover to thwart a group of Albanian terrorists, Victor was kidnapped, tortured and killed as his son watched. Now Noah thinks he can stop agents ever having to go through this again – he can set them free. Living out the fantasy that his father is still alive, a delusional and very sick Noah has set up old socialist sweat Blakeney as the fall guy and led MI5 by the nose.

Noah tells Zoe: 'They don't care about you, you know – you're just a gadget, like the Geiger scrambler.' For Zoe, this will one day turn out to be painfully true. Zoe retorts that, just like his dad, agent Cleopatra is alone in the desert because of his hacking – and will die unless he helps her.

We leave Noah in a psychiatric hospital, playing delusional chess with his dead father. Who enjoins him to '…remember the spider, my boy. When her web is destroyed, what does she do? She spins a new one – even more beautiful…'

SPOOKS 2.4

DIRECTOR: ROB BAILEY

[Scriptwriter: Howard Brenton]

❛ We have to know. We're America. We're trying to run the whole damn planet. **Christine Dale** ❜

Anchored like so many of the scripts in the world of real events, this episode begins with BBC news archive of a Bush–Putin summit in Moscow. The Russian Federation has just been given a $20 billion IMF loan. We cut to the gritty grey tower blocks of the Moscow suburbs. Gangsters make a young Ministry of Finance clerk divulge the account passwords. The $20 billion is transferred to another secret account. They shoot the clerk, and sharp-eyed viewers will notice that leader Viktor Shvitkoy uses the old KGB *vyshaya mera* style of killing – straight through the back of the head.

Back in the UK, there's a separate banking crisis: Bowman Bank employee John Lightwood has stolen $1 billion. Bank of England governor Sir John Barry and Bowman Bank chief Sir Richard 'Dicky' Bowman don't want MI5 officially involved – but, as it happens, Harry Pearce and Dicky are old friends. Amanda 'I'm the chancellor's political counsel' Roake stalks into the meeting late, and starts throwing her weight about.

When Tom objects that catching Lightwood and recovering the money is a job for Scotland Yard, Roake – up there with Whitehall's most unpleasant – squashes him. 'Look: all you have to do is what you're told.' As Harry probes further, it emerges that Bowman and Co. 'handle certain government accounts'.

Danny gets volunteered for the undercover role: 'You have a history of swindling credit cards. I would have thought that makes you perfect for the job. I want to know what they're not telling us about this old family bank.' Malcolm is sent off to bug Banco Co-operativo, home to Lightwood's original money transfer.

Flirting heavily – and as yet unsuccessfully – with Tom to extract what he knows, the CIA's Christine tells him Washington is hyperventilating about the theft of the IMF billions, and suspects Britain.

TOM That's ridiculous.
CHRISTINE Be careful, Tom. We want our money back and if you Brits are holding out on us in some way . . .
TOM No, no, we're just a poor little country out here on the edge of the

American Empire. We wouldn't dream of touching your money.
CHRISTINE Good. You know your place, then.

Danny turns out to be 'a huge talent', not least because Ruth is feeding him secret business information trawled by GCHQ.

Zoe sends Malcolm, the 'Leonardo of the Dustbins', a bag of 'delicious' shredded bank documents. But the mood darkens – and the pace starts to blister – when Lightwood is found crucified on Hampstead Heath. Dishy bad girl and Lightwood ex Maxie Baxter (*right*) joins top trader Danny for loadsamoney celebrations, City-style, at a lap dancing club.

A fellow trader tells Danny that Lightwood was laundering dirty money through Bowman's, 'all the way to Lugano...to the Banco Co-operativo' [Switzerland]. The bank, Ruth discovers, has a permanent suite at the Paramount Hotel, Mayfair, so Tom, Malcolm and Colin go in with the bugs. Ruth notes that Lightwood was crucified Russian mafia-style – ringing a big bell with Tom in light of the missing Moscow millions.

The plot ratchets up when we find out that Sir Richard Bowman is in deep with chief gangster Shvitkoy. Lightwood was meant to have laundered the $1 billion he stole from Bowman and Co., followed in short order by the remaining US billions. Suspecting Bowman may have been in cahoots with Lightwood, Shvitkoy, with characteristic gangster charm, tells him the crucifixion '...was a warning to you. You genitally shrivelled, English bed-pisser.'

Things get murkier still when it appears that Roake is also a part of the money-laundering plot, which now appears to be UK government-inspired and part of some wider plan. Dustbin artist Malcolm discovers that Sir Richard Bowman opened an account for Lightwood on the same day the £1 billion went missing. Harry gives Danny the tough job of seducing Maxie Baxter to find out what's going on.

Furious, Roake orders Harry to back off and remove Danny from the bank or else. When Tom calls her bluff, she stalks out. The problem for MI5 is that if Roake knows about Danny's undercover work, it can only have come from a leak. But who is the mole?

Tom confronts Ruth. 'You betrayed us.' Ruth confesses she always wanted to be a 'real' spy – but was promised the transfer to MI5 only if she 'very occasionally' leaked information. Tom leaves her dangling on probation.

By some strange and horrible coincidence Banco Co-operativo employee Carlo books Zoe for a romantic tryst in the company's Mayfair hotel suite. The one MI5 has bugged. Suddenly, Colin is getting to know Zoe rather more intimately than he ever expected.

Understandably devastated when Tom shows her the revealing surveillance footage, Zoe is even more upset when Tom reveals Carlo is married. Tom has Colin lose the compromising footage – but they

have to know if Carlo is involved in the $20 billion theft.

Zoe has unwittingly handed Tom a trump card – which he doesn't hesitate to use. First, Zoe dumps cheating lover Carlo, then Tom and the boys confront him. When Carlo refuses to name the person controlling the stolen $1 billion, Tom blackmails him with the compromising surveillance stills. Carlo spills the name: Viktor Shvitkoy.

Ruth discovers that Maxie Baxter doesn't just have a false birth certificate – her whole life story is invented.

Harry and Tom now know Russian mafia psychopath Shvitkoy has the money – and guess that Maxie Baxter is his daughter. With Danny set to meet Maxie in two hours' time, Tom demands an explanation for Bowman and Co.'s involvement in the theft. When Shvitkoy first approached Bowman for help in laundering the cash, MI6 asked Bowman to take part in a sting to steal the money back from Shvitkoy. But Lightwood – the chosen conduit – stole the first $1 billion for himself instead, causing the whole infernal mess.

Despite collapsing with a stroke, Bowman – not a traitor, then, but a patriot – manages to pass on the secret account details. Under the baleful gaze of Shvitkoy spy Maxie, Danny now steals the remaining $19 billion back. When Maxie tells Shvitkoy it's happened again, he tells her to 'Stay with him [Danny]. Do anything he wants to do – but get him to tell you where the money is.' Danny is ecstatic with the buzz of stealing $19 billion – until Zoe tells him who Maxie really is. And who her father is.

Danny's flat is bugged and treated to a City-style makeover. Playing the double game as well as he can, Danny tells Maxie Bowman's Bank is laundering $19 billion in stolen money. And he has pinched the lot. Fishing, he tries to do a deal. But Maxie stalls, snoops and finds a gym card in the name of 'Danny Hunter'. The MI5 'cleaners' have let him down. Danny is taken prisoner.

Shvitkoy gives him an ultimatum: 'the money or your eyes'. Danny is about to get a knitting needle through the retinas when Maxie comes in – with a bugged toothpick he planted on her back at his flat. 'See, Viktor,' Danny quips, 'tracker equipment has come on a lot since you were in the KGB.' A stun grenade comes through the wall, followed by the Special Forces rescue team.

Roake thanks Danny and the team for a 'highly satisfactory outcome'. But he will not tell Tom where the money has gone. A further chat with Christine suggests the British Treasury kept the wedge and used it to improve the NHS. The Russian government gets another $20 billion from the USA. And Tom burns the compromising photographs of Zoe and Carlo. Another budding romance gone up in the smoke of the MI5 bonfire . . .

SPOOKS 2.5

DIRECTOR: JUSTIN CHADWICK
[Scriptwriter: Howard Brenton]

> ❝ Because...we may be able to do nothing at all, sweet F.A.,
> as London is destroyed. And that's the reality of being
> under an attack like this. **Tom Quinn** ❞

'When troubles come, they come not single spies.' The first cloud arrives in the form of Tom's latest squeeze Vicky Westbrook – up till now a no-strings-attached breath of fresh air – who demands he go on holiday with her to Egypt. Tom can't visit Egypt for security reasons, the job once again getting in the way of his love life.

Still angry and upset about MI5's intrusion on her affair with Carlo, Zoe finds Sam's shoulder to cry on. But the Major Incident alarm goes off: the spooks are hit with an 'EERIE', or Extreme Emergency Response Exercise. As Bridget Sands and Mark Woolly, 'quizzers from St Alban's', arrive, Danny turns up late and is let in after the doors are officially closed. Harry names Tom 'EMEX' – Emergency Executive Officer – Danny his deputy. They are told there has been an explosion in Parliament Square. The pod doors are sealed: no one in, no one out. Gradually – and brilliantly – what started as an exercise begins to look all too real. All phones and mobiles on the Grid are cut off. Radio and TV news bulletins detail a dirty bomb explosion. The Prime Minister and the Cabinet flee to the 'Turnstile' government bunker in the Cotswolds.

Down in the emergency control room, receptionist Dot pulls all the comms plugs. The Grid is totally cut off from the outside world. Colin voices the increasing fear and doubt we all share: 'What if this isn't a drill?' The scheduled television signal crashes, but the ghostly image of fire-fighter Stephanie swims up on screen, holding cards up that read 'P Square' and 'VX'. VX, Sam tells us, is one of the deadliest nerve agents ever invented, with a human 'LD' or lethal dose of some 10mgs.

Tom now has the terrible decision of ordering Stephanie out of her vehicle to find out what's happening. With her personal air supply exhausted, this is a certain death sentence. 'James Bond behind a desk, getting others to do the dirty work.' Stephanie tells Tom that the van that exploded in Parliament Square had 'Pluto Removals' written on the side.

Ruth points out that Patmos – the name of a terrorist group – is also the name of the Greek island where St John wrote *Revelations* – the book of the end of the world. The Patmos threat is to bomb ten UK cities: 'The British Whore's last breath.'

Zoe now believes – as do we – that the emergency is real. In the pressure-cooker confinement of the Grid, any cracks in character begin to show. Visitors Bridget and Mark are acting up. Ruth suggests they 'just walk out to be with their loved ones'. Tom's veto is final: 'We don't discuss this again.' Danny and Sam declare mutual attraction.

As the satlink goes down, Tom calls a brainstorming session. Mark and Bridget want to move to an Ops room that works. If we were still in any doubt, the Downing Street EMEX, Paul, now tells Tom the emergency is real. The PM, Cabinet and the Royal Family are dead. Despite all pleas, Paul (*right*) cuts the comms link 'to take a walk in St James's Park'.

Mark and Bridget keep up their attack on Tom. Unruffled, Tom tells them to go and collect food. When they argue, Danny backs him up. The remaining water is rationed.

Ruth estimates the death toll from the airborne VX – already one million – will include most of south-east England by nightfall. Harry, who went to the loo before it was closed, has to be quarantined, leaving Tom to run the whole country after handing him the secret 'JIGSAW' protocols. Tom's top priority is to warn the other threatened cities. Confessing he is at a loss, Tom gets no help from Ruth. Tom instructs Edinburgh EMEX John McLeish to evacuate the city, but red tape artist McLeish insists on an order from 'recognised government'.

When the visitors demand access to Harry so they can leave, Tom has to tell them Harry is dying. Mark blames Tom for letting late-as-usual-Danny in when the Grid should have been sealed. Colin rounds on Danny, and they have to be stopped from fighting. Tom makes the pair of them apologise to one another. The character cracks are turning into fault lines.

Mark and Bridget insist they have to go to the Ashford safe house – but Ruth points out the prevailing wind direction means they will certainly die. And kill everyone else when they open the pod doors. With matters growing ever more desperate, Tom asks Zoe for authority to draw weapons: to stop anyone leaving the Grid by force if necessary.

Climbing into protective suits, the visitors announce they are leaving. Tom and Zoe take aim with the pistols. Danny tries to handcuff Mark. When Mark keeps coming, Tom shoots him (*left*).

In a revelation that is almost the equal of St John's, the lights come back up and the fiction is broken. Harry walks out of his office, perfectly well, with a smile on his face. 'Congratulations Tom – a superb display of leadership.' In the midst of relieved laughter, tears and applause for Tom's excellent performance under the most intense pressure, Harry breaks out the champagne.

At which moment Doctor Vicky calls Tom to bawl him out for standing her up. Given what he has just been through, her call could hardly have come at a worse time. 'I can't go on seeing you. It's not working.'

The team goes down The George – MI5's real-life haunt – for a well-earned celebration. As they do, the monitors flash: alert. An attack is imminent...

SPOOKS 2.6

DIRECTOR: JUSTIN CHADWICK
[Scriptwriter: Howard Brenton]

'We'd like paranoia to be the norm here until our Commander-in-Chief is safely back in the skies. Christine Dale '

With President Bush threatening 'pre-emptive strikes' against Iran, newly available Tom and the CIA's Christine fizz and flirt at an Italian Trade reception. The French delegate tells Harry the real reason for Bush's visit is secret negotiations with the Libyans. 'Whose side are you on?' Harry's sharp retort is 'Ours.'

As Tom and Zoe discuss the POTUS [President of the United States] visit, Christine and her sharp-suited CIA colleagues march onto the Grid, demanding total control. Their guys have laptops. Ours have pencil and paper. Winning the turf war with Tom over close Presidential protection, Christine gains total access to the MI5 Registry.

In Christine's takeover, the reality of the UK's so-called 'special relationship' with America could hardly be better scrutinised – or satirised: 'Every rumour is to be treated as fact until neutralised. We'd like paranoia to be the norm here until our Commander-in-Chief is back in the skies.' Zoe asks the glaring question: if he's supposed to be on such a tight schedule, then why is Bush going 'sightseeing'?

With Danny's help, Sam just manages to stop Christine spotting a US diplomatic crate UK Customs have opened by accident, in breach of diplomatic protocol. The US diplomatic pouches in the crate are soaked in the Customs' guy's spilled tea. Still, it's an opportunity: Malcolm can trawl through them for evidence of Bush's secret meeting with the Libyans – and get rid of the tea stains – all in the next eighteen hours.

As if they didn't already have enough on their plates, the spooks are up for their annual psychological assessment. Danny loses the toss with Zoe and has to go in first with Miranda – aka 'Inspector Freud'.

Pointing out that Britain's entry in the CIA fact book reads, 'Slightly smaller than Oregon', Tom punctures Christine's patronising pep talk about 'working together':

TOM That's what we are to you – slightly smaller than Oregon ... Don't think you can just order us around, OK?
CHRISTINE He's our president.
TOM It's our country.

At the end of a very funny staring match between Danny and Miranda, Danny makes a flip comment about 'The Weirdo [public access] Line'. Miranda uses the mistake as a lever: she wants him to talk about working with Zoe.

To his huge annoyance, jilted Doctor Vicky keeps calling Tom. And won't accept he has dumped her.

A strange man waiting outside Tom's home calls him by his real name, Tom Quinn. Vengeful Vicky has distributed leaflets advertising his services as a male prostitute: 'On Her Majesty's Sexy Service.' Tom gets so many calls from potential clients Zoe has to change all his phone numbers. Under threat of dismissal for the security breach, a highly embarrassed Tom presents the changes as a 'routine security check'.

While Sam goes round Soho discreetly taking down all the sex leaflets, a ham radio hacker discovers Airforce One's scheduled route and landing time. Internet postings mean there is a real potential threat to POTUS. Tom and Christine argue over its seriousness until, making a direct appeal for his backing, Christine wins Tom's agreement to her proposed security changes.

Citing a supposed criticism of her, Miranda sows dissent between Zoe and Danny, who start bickering in the middle of the POTUS security run-through.

Challenging him about the fact he changed his cell phone number in the middle of a live op, Christine realises Tom has a problem.

Increased Libyan Embassy chatter cements the view that Bush is in London to broker a side deal with the Libyans over Lockerbie – that doesn't include the British.

Tom fails to notice Vicky tailing him, even though she picks him up right outside Thames House. Christine notices. Especially when Vicky embarrasses Tom horribly at the Horseguards security walk-through. Forcing Tom to explain on the grounds that it is now a CIA matter, Christine insists on helping him deal with it. And warns Tom any further gruesomes like the compromising sex leaflets will cost him his job.

Ruth spreads the rumour that someone on the Grid is getting the sack having failed psychological assessment, hugely increasing the in-house paranoia factor.

Now comes an odd, unexplained and apparently unauthorised change to the President's schedule. While the spooks speculate this is part of his cover for the Libya talks, CIA heavies abduct Doctor Vicky from her hospital – nicely tapping along the theme that the real nature of Britain's 'special relationship' is one of abject inferiority. While the CIA trash Vicky's flat, a scary Christine warns her to leave Tom alone – or else.

With Chequers besieged by anti-Bush protestors and Special Branch snipers on the roof, Tom, Danny and Christine take control inside – only to have RAF radar warn of a slow-moving contact coming right at the house. Back on the Grid, Zoe flags up a surveillance shot of known Russian hitman Dmitri Bubka, taken the day before. Bubka has been trying to buy a radiotherapy machine which Ruth points out contains enough Cobalt 60 to make a dirty bomb.

The CIA, in the teeth of Tom's repeated objections, orders the Harriers to shoot down the microlight. With the Harriers seconds from opening fire, the microlight turns away. Christine leaves the final call to Tom: 'Negative...target is no longer a threat.' He's right – the pilot turns out to have a defective radio – 'and a defective head'.

Tom has to yell to make the Grid believe no one is getting the sack. Told that most of the negative comments in the assessment are about him, Tom throws the attack in Miranda's face: 'I think I'm looking at the weakest link right now.'

Asking him to return the US diplomatic crate as a means of returning the favour she did Tom, Christine flatly denies any US–Libyan contact. Watching the video recording of the US President meeting the Libyan negotiator – thoughtfully provided by the Libyans – prompts Harry to quote the Bible: 'You shall know the truth and the truth shall set you free.' [John 8:32]

Back home, Christine, in siren mode, invites Tom over to meet her friend Jim [Beam]. Over heavily ironic TV footage of Bush and Blair speechifying about the 'special relationship', Christine and Tom form a new and very special bond of their own.

SPOOKS 2.7

DIRECTOR: CIARAN DONNELLY

[Scriptwriter: Simon Mirren]

> We must task a completely deniable agent. A cleanskin.
> Win or lose, there can be nothing to trace them back to us.
> Tom Quinn

Stuck in commuter traffic, Harry gets back home to find a gang of armed and masked burglars have broken into his house using a homemade but extremely advanced alarm killer. And they've stolen the crucial briefcase Harry should never have taken home. One of the raiders has left a tell-tale pool of blood on the floor.

Backed by UK arms dealer Frank Hastings, 'French military scientist with an ego the size of the Eiffel Tower' Henri Durand has resigned from a top-secret French military project. And he's taken 'Firestorm', the cutting edge Electro-magnetic Pulse [EMP] air-burst missile blueprints with him. With MI6 monitoring the case, MI5's task is to steal the technology from Hastings, Durand and the French before it's sold on. And they must do it under the nose of hunky French Secret Service agent Jean-Luc Guion, without getting caught. The spooks need the help of a 'cleanskin' – someone with no prior connection to MI5.

TOM The key to procuring Firestorm is Durand's laptop.
ZOE Firestorm's like a jigsaw. It's encrypted on the web in numerous sites. The only way to complete the jigsaw is with a series of codes, which must be inputted on Durand's computer.
TOM MI6 have tried to access the laptop before.
ZOE Tried and failed. They did, however, discover the access codes via surveillance recordings.
TOM looks across the faces of his team.
DANNY And where are these codes?
ZOE It's alright. Harry's got them in his briefcase.

Oops. Meanwhile, locked permanently to Durand's wrist or in a safe, only one copy of the Firestorm blueprints exist. Guion's dashing Gallic looks set the female spooks fighting over him. So Tom wisely tasks Danny with the Anglo-French liaison job.

JJ – the youngest of Harry's burglars – has a photographic memory. His friend Kyle tells JJ he's 'special' and could do better if his big brother Denton wasn't holding him back.

Convinced the burglary was out of the ordinary – how could an ordinary gang of London crims bypass his extraordinary, Colin-created security? – Harry plays for time to try to save his career. Tom backs Harry. But there are mutterings on the Grid: Ruth, Zoe and Danny fear they will all go down with him if they help cover up.

Dissing the 'worthless' papers in Harry's briefcase, Denton burns them. But not before JJ has idly scanned – and memorised – the pages.

As Sam flirts madly with him, sex-bomb agent Jean-Luc tells the team that Firestorm 'belongs' to France. Debating whether to own up and get the Firestorm codes from MI6, Harry admits there's no way back from his mistake. To make things worse, a rather Bond-like experimental mobile phone gun was also in the case.

The DNA from the blood found on Harry's floor identifies a certain Jason James Franks – JJ [Heshima Thompson]. Toying with the 'ordinary' mobile phone he's found in the case, JJ accidentally shoots his friend Kyle in the chest.

Facing down the burglars – guns and all – Tom and Harry persuade Denton to let them take JJ with them. The prospect of a life sentence if he doesn't comply convinces Denton to co-operate. But he also knows his brother should aim for higher things.

As Ruth and the team spot a Chinese team in Britain to buy Firestorm, Harry faces up to reality. 'Firestorm tips the scales – it outweighs the risks of anything we might lose, and that includes my job. My time is up, I have to come clean. You make a mistake, you pay the price, those are the rules.' His meeting with the DG at 4 p.m. increases the pressure for a result.

Behind everyone's back Guion instructs a second French agent to steal the Firestorm disc and kill Durand.

Tom asks JJ to help. Failing which, he'll go back inside. But JJ hits back: 'Either charge me, or let me see my lawyer, government man.' Entranced – as we all are – by JJ's feisty brilliance, Harry proposes using him as a 'cleanskin' to steal the Firestorm data. Zoe objects, but Harry's right: JJ's their only chance. Tom starts preparing him, but the teenager – who has pickpocketed Zoe's card and memorised the door code – walks out.

They know just where to find him. In a poignant moment, Denton pushes JJ away for his own good. 'Whatever these people want, give it to 'em. Without me, you could fly. Show them the magic.' Desolate, JJ gives himself up to the waiting Tom and Zoe.

Ruth flags up the covert meet between Jean-Luc and fellow French agent Richard Bertrand. The race against the French team is on.

Using a computer model of its interior, Colin and the team coach JJ to make entry into Hastings Defence and steal the Firestorm data. JJ is an exceptionally able pupil, but he has only five minutes before the building's alarm goes off. Realising he has no back-up, no escape route and that MI5 will disown him if he gets caught, JJ asks for – and gets – the truth from Tom: 'You, or anybody else … we leave no traces.'

Armed with a fake access fingerprint provided by Colin, JJ gets in. Zoe's CCTV monitoring breaks down, owing to French interference, and JJ is on his own. He works his 'magic' on a keypad entry system MI5 did not spot. He gets to the Firestorm computer, takes it and drops out of sight when he hears someone coming. Durand appears, followed by a French agent dressed as a security guard. Even if he wanted to, Durand can't hand the laptop over – JJ has it. The agent shoots Durand dead.

Harry and Tom accuse Jean-Luc of conspiring to kill Durand. Jean-Luc counters: MI5 tried to steal Firestorm too. 'Durand didn't manage to sell Firestorm. So like you, the Chinese are left empty-handed. But Bravo – nice try.' Pros to the last, Jean-Luc and Tom shake hands.

The operation's real winner, JJ, last seen locked in a top-security building, has Firestorm and now he's standing outside Thames House, staring at the CCTV camera. Tom and JJ horse-trade on the Embankment (*left*):

JJ Seems I got something you want.
TOM Seems you do.
JJ 'How much do you want it?
TOM Depends on what you think it's worth.
JJ Kyle gets his fruit bowl. Your boss doesn't press charges …
And I get half of this. [*He means £1,500 – half the laptop's value.*]
TOM I can offer you more than money. I can offer you a chance to change your life.
JJ I don't want to change my life. This is my life.

Refusing the offer of education – and a certain job at the end of it – JJ disappears back into the South London wilderness. But he does have Tom's phone number – just in case.

SPOOKS 2.8

DIRECTOR: CIARAN DONNELLY

[Scriptwriter: Stephen Baile]

'Satire never brought a country down. **Harry Pearce**'

As a new winter of discontent threatens to paralyse the country, reports have reached MI5 that a crack army unit may be planning to lead the British Army in a mutiny. Unit member Corporal Woods names his superior officer Major Samuel Curtis as the ringleader.

Working in deep cover at Stonefield Barracks as Lt. Getty, Tom is already on the case. But is the threat from Curtis, a national hero, real? Zoe doesn't think so. Itemising the ways in which a mutiny would embarrass the government, Harry insists they find out.

Zoe ['If we went on strike, I don't think anyone would notice'] sketches a Curtis biog. that echoes the Gulf War I 'Bravo Two Zero' mission. Summoned by a tradecrafty red drawing pin signal, Woods tries to convince a sceptical Tom that Curtis is 'moving his pieces into place' by reassembling his old team from Desert Storm.

Tom doesn't really like 'doing' military. Still, he's making the best of the extra training and some breathing space from Harry, who has banned him from seeing CIA siren Christine. Before calling in at the prearranged time, he sweeps his quarters with a bug-detecting mobile. Danny IDs Curtis's Desert Storm team: Sgt. Maj. Baker, Sgts. Wallace, Hanson and Scobey and Corporal Parkes. Hanson and Scobey have left the army, and Danny chases them up as leads.

Zoe warns Harry that a consignment of spent nuclear fuel on its way to Dover by rail is about to grind to a halt in open countryside. Nothing is sacred when it comes to strikes.

Helping a soldier whose defective respirator fails, Tom tries to convince Curtis he is onside by complaining about useless rifles, shoddy kit etc. Surprisingly, Curtis shuts him up.

Danny poses as journalist Rob Simkins to interview Hanson. Hanson hates Curtis, whose book about the escape from Iraq got him fired from the SAS: 'You can't have a special ops soldier whose face has been on the front page of every Western newspaper.' But in a leading aside, he adds: 'I told him, I'm a soldier, not a bloody chauffeur.' When Danny pushes him, Hanson has a go, forcing Danny to break cover.

Zoe painstakingly sets out a contingency plan to transport the highly irradiated – and stranded – uranium fuel by low-loader convoy. Codenamed 'The Stick', this entails a minimum eight-hour road journey.

But if Dover docks close, the convoy risks being stranded for twenty-four hours. CIA Christine comes at Zoe, trying to get in touch with Tom.

Tasked by Curtis to check Tom out, Wallace calls at Tom's cover 'home' and talks to his fictitious father. The back-up team has been thorough – Tom's cover stands up.

The Stick convoy starts off. 'Hardly the *Wacky Races*, is it?'

A very disaffected Tom tells the Grid that maligned hero Curtis is not a threat. 'Listen to his voicemail. I want to be extracted from this badly sourced, pig's-ear of an operation.' But Malcolm finds access to the voicemail is PIN-protected. With the dockers set to strike at 1900 hours that same evening, The Stick – and the spooks – come under increased pressure.

A sleeping Tom is dragged out of bed and interrogated as Curtis watches. It's 'an exercise'. Stalwart to the last, Tom withstands it (*right*). But nasty informant Corporal Woods, who is next, spills the beans before they have even asked him a question, placing Tom in serious jeopardy.

With his mobile damaged, Tom misses his routine check-in call, triggering the contingency plan: Danny goes in to extract him. Still convinced that Curtis is a good man, Tom couldn't be more wrong. Curtis has them arrested and put on a truck. 'You people screwed up your chance to defend the West. Now it's down to us, the army, to sort it out.'

Malcolm discovers the voice on Curtis's mobile originated at The Stick's start point. Ruth checks the Nuclear Authority database, and comes up with a photo-match for Scobey: he's a plant, one of The Stick's drivers. Zoe's 'routine' convoy re-routing is suddenly a Grade One emergency. She raises the alarm but it's too late – Curtis and his men ambush The Stick and park it up in an oil storage depot ten miles from the centre of London. With Tom and Danny as hostages.

Curtis delivers his ultimatum: unless the government does something about Gulf War Syndrome, inferior weapons and army conditions, the block of plastic explosive [PE] stuck to an oil storage tank will explode. 'If my terms are still not met within sixty minutes – then south-east England will be twinned with Chernobyl.'

Tom tries to reason with the war hero: 'You won't do it.'

'What choice do I have? Your presence here pretty much makes my case for me. Seems that third world and Eastern Bloc dictators are not the only ones who monitor their military.'

Touché. Ouch, even. Using the pretext of a fractured gas main, Zoe orders a 20-km evacuation zone around the depot. The Counter-terrorist [CT] team choppers in and sets up with Barrett Browning. 50 sniper rifles. Harry, too, tries to talk Curtis down. Unaware of the sniper's red laser dot playing on his chest, Curtis brags: 'There isn't a British soldier alive who'd take a shot on me.' Cue the kill shot – Harry's call – and the cover up, in which 'hero' Curtis supposedly died in a car accident.

Christine wants Tom: 'My place, later?' But Harry puts his foot down:

TOM Personal feelings. I have personal feelings . . .

HARRY Then bury them. Because—

TOM Screw. You. If the new world order means we're in the business of destroying anyone who questions the political agenda . . . then I'm in the wrong job. [*A long beat.*]

HARRY Take a long weekend. Then put this operation behind you.

TOM Shame on you, Harry. Shame on you for allowing us to be manipulated.

HARRY (*steel*) 'It's OVER. I'll take your debrief another time. And as regards Mata Hari out there—

CHRISTINE is watching from the Grid.

HARRY —no fraternising with foreign operatives, even if they're friendlies. You and I both know there's no such thing in our world.

TOM I will not—

HARRY NEVER! QUESTION! MY! DECISIONS!

TOM's face is set in stone.

HARRY End it. I don't care how, I do care when. Next time I see you, you're a single man.

He slams the door as he goes.

SPOOKS 2.9

DIRECTOR: SAM MILLER

[Scriptwriter: Ben Richards]

' Good idea, Ruth...Let's leave everyone alone, give every
snake what it wants, then the world can be one big happy
nest of vipers...Tom Quinn '

It's night. Tom is being 'Pete' on a stake-out operation, swapping
notes on kids and football with Jenny, a Customs and Excise colleague:

TOM Joe? Is he any good?
JENNY (*laughs*) Truthfully? He's absolute crap. But he loves it so
I tell him he's the next Thierry Henry. You've got kids, haven't you?
TOM Zoe and Danny. Zoe's in hospital. Her operation must have just
finished. I've promised her lots of ice-cream for being brave.

Tom slips out to 'take a leak' and calls in his status report to the Grid.
When he gets back, the men and women he's just been chatting to have
all been garrotted. Certain the killers must have had insider help, Tom –
in deep shock – gets Ruth to run checks on everyone who knew about
the drugs cartel op.

After Spain deported two cartel members to Colombia, the Chala
cartel planted a reprisal bomb, killing thirty teenagers in a Spanish
disco. 'So we give London to the Chala cartel,' is increasingly
disenchanted Tom's laconic comment, 'or they turn Bournemouth
into Bali.'

The action ratchets up when the Home Office tells the spooks to
make the war on drugs their top priority. And on the personal front,
when Harry reminds Tom to break off his love affair with Christine.

Placing cartel boss Rafa Morrientes and girlfriend Mariela Hernandez
under twenty-four-hour surveillance, MI5 watch the couple meet Ross
Vaughan, finance director of the UK's top oil company PETCAL. PETCAL
wants to build a Colombian oil pipeline through cartel territory.

Key go-between Mariela goes under the microscope. Surveillance
king Danny turns up Chala cartel members working as cleaners inside
PETCAL's HQ: Vaughan is hiding a cartel cell in the basement. Danny's
task is to find one of the cleaners with an Achilles heel – and use it.

In the meantime, Zoe catches Sam – who has been behaving
mysteriously – fiddling with a palmtop on the Grid. She claims it is
a gift from a friend.

Christine's response to being told Harry's banned their affair is that they should cheat. After all, they are spooks.

Danny spots Mariela swapping briefcases with Vaughan: they need to find out what's inside. Tom and Zoe work up their 'Katie and Jack' brother and sister legends. She's in publishing, he's a risk analyst – '...slightly aloof; cold, even. I never know what you're thinking...' The story for orphaned Mariela is that their own parents were killed when they were young. Zoe chats her up in the gym, takes their target for a coffee – and Tom just happens to turn up.

Getting seriously proactive, Tom and Danny lift Chala cartel goon Camillo. His mother is in prison: they will get her out if he will agree to help Danny infiltrate the cartel. Camillo shows Danny – now working as a cleaner at PETCAL's HQ – the basement meeting room. What Danny really wants to find is the cartel's armoury. More goons arrive as Danny finishes installing a bug in a light bulb. They would have caught Danny red-handed – if, in a sparky reference to Ian Fleming's *Goldfinger*, he hadn't been hiding in the roof beams.

Ruth shows Harry the bug transcript: the cartel wants to trade drugs for Surface-to-Air Missiles [SAMs]. Great. Dead set against Harry's plan to intercept the deal early, Tom wants to let it run.

Zoe sets up an 'accidental' coffee spill that allows an officer to grab Mariela's case, photograph its contents and then return it. In return for his mother's parole and new identities in the USA, Danny persuades a frightened Camillo to plant a tracking device on the SAMs.

The briefcase contains bearer bonds and Shell company shares used to launder drugs money. Vaughan is the linchpin, using PETCAL as cover for importing drugs, then laundering the cash from their sale.

Bonding with Zoe and Tom over a glass of wine and a bout of salsa dancing, Mariela responds to their invented tragic childhood tale with her own, real one: her whole family was murdered. Her mother had given Mariela and her father identical rings and the killers stole his.

Furious when he finds out she has had company, Rafa warns Mariela – who is effectively his prisoner – against making the same mistake. 'It would be better for whoever this girl is if you didn't see her again. Do you understand me?' We do.

Zoe questions the callous way in which the spooks are using Mariela. 'Unpleasant? Morally questionable? That's the world we live in, really,' Tom retorts.

Zoe finds out why Sam has been acting so suspiciously: tricky old Tessa has gulled her into passing information from the Grid. The palmtop was being used to download information from computer files. As a result, Tessa knows all about Tom's affair with Christine – and, much more seriously, details of the anti-Chala op. Engineering a meet with

Zoe, she proposes a deal: let her 'clients' in Spain – she means the Spanish Secret Service – dispose of Rafa afterwards, and she will give MI5 information that will help turn Mariela (*right*). 'That woman has the morality of a puff adder,' says Harry.

Tessa's info reveals it was actually Rafa who killed Mariela's family – and then took her as a war trophy while posing as her saviour. To make Mariela believe this, MI5 needs more convincing proof. Tom suggests they 'find' – i.e. remake – her dead father's ring. Breaking cover, Tom and Zoe pick Mariela up, explain who they are and show her a box which they say is from Rafa's hotel room. Her father's ring is inside. With Zoe promising they will look after her, Mariela bites.

Ruth tells Harry that Sam is Tessa's mole. Dredging up his brutal side, Harry gives Sam a rough time to get her to talk. But Sam – duped by Tessa into believing she is taking part in an exercise organised by 'Jane in training' – only does so when a fax supposedly ending her ordeal comes through: 'The bar is open.'

Harry loses it. He gets Tessa's Spanish security contacts to cut her out of the payment loop – otherwise they don't get Rafa and their revenge for the disco bomb. Tom and Harry are at odds again over what to do with Mariela. Tom wants to catch Vaughan, Harry wants to let him go. Winning the argument, Tom asks Mariela to wear a wire to entrap Vaughan.

The trap is set. They get Vaughan on tape boasting that Rafa couldn't get his drugs into the country without his friends in government and Customs and Excise. But he wants sex in return for naming names.

Tessa gets her questionable revenge on Harry by telling Vaughan that Mariela is a traitor. In the resulting showdown, when Rafa has pulled a knife on her, Mariela takes a strange and brave stand, taunting Rafa about the sex with Vaughan: ' It was better than with you. I was screaming with pleasure.' Rafa stabs her.

Too late, a DVD message arrives from Tessa: she has blown Mariela's cover and is on the run.

So much for the promise of protection. Tom holds Mariela as she dies, and mourns the passing of his own soul. But the scythe is coming for Rafa, too: MI5 officers hand him over to their Spanish counterparts – who promptly garrotte him. Special Operations Director Tim Allardyce – the cartel informer responsible for the eight Customs deaths – will at the very least lose his pension. Sam gets a second chance. But Vaughan, protected by sources at the heart of the British government, escapes justice. Harry appears to condone this, on the grounds that they took out the cartel and its weapons. Tom is scathing, detailing the gruesome way in which Rafa killed Mariela. Desolate, disgusted and damned, Tom takes comfort in Christine's arms. We doubt he will find a cure.

SPOOKS 2.10

DIRECTOR: SAM MILLER

[Scriptwriter: Howard Brenton]

> ❛ I hate this loyalty thing. It tears you apart...Danny Hunter ❜

Watching one of the best films ever made, *The Third Man*, professional assassin Mickey 'The Shark' Karharias finds himself looking down the barrel in his Miami home. Someone powerful wants Karharias to carry out a hit on an Englishman. The catch is, they want him to do it dead.

In bed with Tom Quinn, Christine Dale shows him a Top Secret CIA telex she believes was delivered to her desk by mistake (*left*). The telex details a plot originating in the Middle East to have Karharias kill a British VIP in London. It ends, 'Action decided: Extreme Weather. Do not advise mice.' 'Extreme Weather' is CIA code for a clandestine op to 'desensitise' – assassinate – an individual on foreign soil. The 'mice' are MI5.

For all the right reasons, Christine felt she had to tell Tom. And he wants to keep her safe. But a menacing spook – 'Flat Cap' – watches Tom leave the hotel.

Tom tells Zoe and Danny about the upcoming CIA hit on British soil. He also tells them he can't tell Harry, so Zoe guesses the info came from Christine. Our mounting worry over Tom's state of mind increases with his question: 'Zoe, sometimes don't you find that you just want to turn this job inside out, just break all the rules?' To stop the hit, Tom orders a stakeout at Heathrow arrivals: the CIA Cland-ops team will follow Karharias – and they'll follow the CIA.

Unhappy about not making the mission official, Zoe works on Danny: 'We have to tell Harry...The target could be the Prime Minister.' Then Danny spots a CIA surveillance team. Recognising Flat Cap, Tom assumes he is a CIA spook watching Christine. And then – confusingly – Karharias arrives. Tom has a simple plan: tail Karharias to his lair, call Harry and send in the cavalry. Two problems: the first, Flat Cap spots Tom; second, Danny finds their car tyres slashed.

Since his entanglement with Christine, Zoe has replaced Tom as the CIA liaison officer. At their meet, Zoe – who suspects Christine may be setting Tom up – demands the original telex as proof there really is a Cland-ops hit in progress. Christine can't produce the telex: Tom burned it. Not only that, the only reason Christine can give for not recognising Flat Cap as CIA is that, 'He's Cland-ops. His cover will be very deep. What is this, an interrogation?' More concerned than ever, Zoe gets in Tom's face: 'Tell Harry...'

'I will – soon.'

When Danny stands by Tom, Zoe is blunt:

ZOE I'm afraid he's losing it over this, and will drag me into trouble.
DANNY Us. Us into trouble.

Though equally worried, Tom is cool: 'My skin's crawling about it too.
It's a feeling you come to rely on in this job.' Malcolm gives Tom
a tiny CIA-developed nano tracking device that can be planted with
a fingertip and controlled from a laptop.

Danny follows Tom into 'A–Z Leather' – a warehouse filled with creepy
mannequins. Cracking the office safe, Danny finds an Irish passport
in the name of 'Paul Conners'. With a Slovakian visa. Tom's photograph.
And a stash of cash. It looks as if Tom is preparing an illegal legend –
and means to abscond.

Discovering what has been going on behind his back, Harry comes
close to having Danny and Zoe skinned.

Introducing himself as Herb Ziegler, Flat Cap patronises Tom on his
home turf (*right*): the CIA doesn't mind his 'kind of sweet' affair with
Christine. It does mind Tom interfering with the hit. Menace and
mutual contempt.

Tom squares up to him:

ZIEGLER Let the big boys do what they've got to do. And Christine
won't get hurt. (*A beat.*)
TOM Do I have a choice?
ZIEGLER No.

When he goes out to take a phone call, Tom sticks the nano tracking
device on Ziegler's briefcase, skips out the back to avoid Harry, starts
tracking Ziegler and calls Zoe and Danny for backup. Now they're into
a very atmospheric *Third Man*-style flash-frame sequence: Ziegler as
Harry Lime and Tom naïvely blundering after him, like Holly Martins
in the classic film. Sparks shower from the overhead rail line. Tom
photographs Ziegler's dead-drop message. 'Our friend is warned off –
where's the meet?' it reads.

Tom convinces Zoe and Danny to stick with it and not call Harry:
'For God's sake, this is the only lead we've got to stop an assassination.
Come on, nights like this, you love it, you know you do! That's why we
do the job.'

Three hours later, Ziegler's contact turns up, reads the note and
leaves a new one: 'Salter's Farm, Feniston, near Sudbury.' Tom has to
convince Zoe yet again: 'What the CIA are doing is espionage as rape:
they are trying to destroy my personal life with Christine. Why should

I trust them with my country?' Presuming dangerously once more on their friendship, Tom asks Danny and Zoe to choose: 'Are you for me or against me?' Choosing for Tom, they go with him to the farm and walk straight into Ziegler's trap.

With his three best spooks missing, Harry's beside himself. Sam keeps trying to raise them. Ruth gives Harry the FBI tip-off that Karharias is in reality dead. That does it:

HARRY I think Tom Quinn's on the blink … He's been running an op on his own for his own purposes and I'm having nightmares about what they are.
RUTH Harry, Tom Quinn is your brightest and best.
HARRY It's the brightest and the best who can go bad so spectacularly.
RUTH What are you going to do?
HARRY Issue a warrant for Tom Quinn's arrest. The police will pick him up on an anti-terrorism charge.

The trap unfolds. Strung up by the arms with Tom and Zoe in a remote barn (*left*), Danny is the first to be interrogated. When he won't tell Ziegler what he knows about Tom they hood Danny and beat him. Zoe goes in next – but not Tom. Why not Tom? Danny confronts Tom about the secret 'Paul Connors' legend. Tom explains he was checking out the 'A–Z Leather' logo on Ziegler's carrier bag at the Heathrow stakeout. But Danny no longer believes Tom. Especially when Tom is released.

Ziegler's men drug Danny and Zoe, who wake up the next morning free and go back in to Thames House. Danny tells Harry he thinks Tom, in cahoots with Ziegler, has set up whole thing: Karharias at Heathrow, the farm, the A–Z Leather legend, all of it. Harry believes Tom must be controlling the upcoming assassination. But even when Ruth finds $4 million in a newly created bank account in the name of 'Paul Connors', Zoe refuses to believe Tom is a traitor.

Interrogating Christine, Harry lays it bare: there is no CIA record of the telex she showed Tom, nor of any accompanying satellite intercept. The telex was sent from a commercial address in London and not the Middle East, Karharias is dead and Christine has Slovakian parentage, which ties in with Tom's visa. Spurning his offer of help if she comes clean, Christine protests she has no idea what Harry is talking about.

Tom wakes up to find himself holding a Gepard sniper rifle. Then gets a kick in the face. Herb Ziegler is in reality ex-CIA agent Hermann Joyce – 'one of the living dead'. His daughter, Lisa, is in a facility in Maine in a catatonic state. For which he blames Tom Quinn.

Back in the days when Tom and Lisa were both students, Joyce asked Tom to help him get Lisa out of the clutches of a radical anarchist group:

TOM I warned her off them, as you asked me.
JOYCE Don't be so disingenuous, you little shit. You recruited her! You turned her into a Five asset, an untrained girl of nineteen. You sent her undercover to penetrate a hardcore European anarchist cell.
TOM It was her choice!
JOYCE You know what they did when they discovered her? They tortured her for five days.
TOM It was her choice.

Tom blacks out. When he wakes, he walks to a private house and calls in to warn the Grid there is going to be a hit in the Ipswich area. Too late – the Chief of the Defence Staff has been shot dead. Tom tries to explain that he has been set up by Joyce – and asks for a meet. Zoe – still struggling to keep her faith in Tom – finds out the story about Lisa Joyce is true.

Agreeing to meet Tom – with Special Forces on standby – Harry asks Ruth to check out Joyce on the US agency databases. When Harry, Zoe and Danny arrive at the rendezvous, Tom, holding a shotgun, tries to clear his name. Hermann Joyce has set him up. Zoe points out that Joyce died five years before in a car crash.

Tom has run out of road. As Harry triggers the call button, Tom shoots him and runs for it. He makes it to the beach, walks into the sea and starts swimming. As the medics take Harry – wounded in the shoulder – for treatment, the call to Danny's mobile suggests the police have found a body in the sea. But the story leaves us hanging – is Tom alive? Arrested? Or has he committed suicide?

THE THIRD MAN
Written by Graham Greene and directed by the brilliant Carol Reed, *The Third Man* (1949) is about lots of things, but mostly naïvety, deceit and betrayal. Set in post-war Vienna, cinematographer Robert Krasker gave it an expressionist world-weary look, with harsh lighting and distorted camera angles. His style is plainly referred to in several key scenes: director of photography Sue Gibson clearly had a good time on this one. Tom is of course, the 'Third Man'. Think about it: Tom now plays dead, after Hermann Joyce pretended to be dead; having killed Karharias, who was watching the film. And is dead.

SPOOKS 3.1

DIRECTOR: JONNY CAMPBELL
[Scriptwriter: Howard Brenton]

' There is speculation that the suspect drowned on the Suffolk coast while trying to escape. Police have cordoned off all nearby beaches. Newsreader '

With Tom missing, presumed traitorous assassin, MI5 is in crisis – and at the mercy of the JIC [Joint Intelligence Committee] Chairman Oliver Mace. Ex-desk spook and arch-bully Mace tells the stunned team: 'I am launching an investigation. Sanctioned by Downing Street. So you are all suspended. This is going to be something of a bloodbath.'

MI5 is fighting for its very survival.

As the suspended Danny, Zoe, Sam and Ruth gather in informal war council in the tube station, a 'vagrant' comes up to warn them they are all being bugged and watched. This is our first sighting of the alarmingly handsome Adam Carter. Danny and Zoe try to reach Christine Dale, but Christine, suspected of helping Tom kill the Chief of the Defence Staff in episode 2.10 – and stay on the run – is being fried under the CIA grill.

A wounded but defiant Harry arrives back on the Grid to confront Mace, who has already been interrogating and threatening to fire everyone. With MI5 looking down the JIC barrel, Adam Carter strides in through the pods like the answer to a Grid prayer. He's been 'wangled' from '6' to help save the day. Adam has the same plan as Danny – prove Tom Quinn's innocence, and get MI5 off the hook.

Strolling under the symbolic dinosaurs of the Natural History Museum, Harry's former colleague and JIC ally tells him the bad news: Downing Street weasel Jason Belling wants to create a single intelligence agency controlled centrally from Number Ten. 'Our very own KGB', Harry spits. At this crucial moment filthy, smelly, living-rough Tom Quinn calls Harry to say he can prove his innocence. Harry wants to know how.

TOM I've got a way.
HARRY You are a dead man in the North Sea, and you will remain so until proved otherwise.

Tom does have a way. Hermann Joyce's daughter, Lisa, was a devout Catholic. Tom bets that Joyce – who set him up – will pay one last sentimental visit to her favourite church. When Joyce appears, Tom wins the short, brutal fight. Holding him at gunpoint, Tom tries to take him in. But Joyce – who blames him for Lisa's insanity – won't be taken. However, Tom doesn't need Joyce alive to prove his innocence. Shooting Joyce, Tom dumps the body outside Thames House.

Hermann Joyce taunts Tom into shooting him in London's most exquisite parish church, St Bartholomew-the-Great, founded, together with the famous hospital Bart's, by Rahere, Henry I's court jester. Henry VIII demolished much of it during the Reformation, but it is still one of the most spiritual of London's many secret treasures.

To get right off the JIC hook, MI5 needs incontrovertible proof. Was Joyce's wife and fellow spy Carmen in on the conspiracy? Turning up at Danny and Zoe's flat, Tom suggests using Joyce's phone to entrap Carmen, who doesn't yet know that her husband is dead. Adam fleshes out the plan: send Carmen a text message on Joyce's phone, set up a London rendezvous, grab her and extract the truth on the record. Harry: 'So we lure a US citizen to this country and force a confession out of her. That is a totally illegal, madcap scheme – I like it, Adam.'

Going for the weak spot, Mace bullies Christine into betraying Tom (*right*). Lying about the fact she's wearing a wire linked to Mace, Christine persuades Tom to tell her where MI5 plans to lift Carmen.

Not for the first time, the enemy is within. Waiting in the hotel lobby, Zoe spots Mace's 'goons' loitering with intent to grab Carmen first. With Adam and Danny's help, she spikes them. Carmen makes a run for it, texting her husband's mobile – which Malcolm has – to say she is 'on the way to the safe house'. At this chaotic point MI5 might have lost Carmen if she hadn't hailed one of the 'spook taxis' Ruth has recruited on the quiet. Racing to the address, Harry calls for armed backup.

With Special Forces in position, Colin and Danny fibre-optic Carmen's room. They find her loading a pistol. Burning to get the truth out of Carmen himself, Tom locks horns with Adam, who gets the job instead on Harry's insistence. And what a job he does, telling Carmen the plain truth: her husband is dead. Convinced this is a terminal mistake, Harry wants to send in the troops. But Tom stays his hand – it's exactly what he would have said.

Adam spins Carmen a winning tale about Joyce taking five agents with him in a big shoot-out with MI5. Wanting to believe it, Carmen does believe it. Seeing his edge, Adam spoons on the flattery:

ADAM Setting up Tom was a great scam.
CARMEN More. It had elegance. Are we bugged?
ADAM Of course.
CARMEN And you're asking me to confess?
ADAM Yes.

In an echo of *From Russia With Love* Carmen reveals that the operation to set Tom up was financed out of Damascus by Iraqi Baathists. 'They wanted a big assassination in England [the Chief of the Defence Staff] and we saw the chance to set up the patriotic English spy as the killer.'

Carmen's taped confession completely exonerates Tom. Which means Harry's dinner that night will be humble pie. 'We all misjudged you so much – I'm so very sorry.' Tom's reply gives a hint of what he's been through during his forty days and forty nights in the wilderness: 'It's like it's stopped raining in my head.'

Carmen puts the pistol in her mouth and blows her brains out. In a wonderful closing scene at their club, Oliver Mace and Harry Pearce hang the scheming Jason Belling out to dry. Harry still has a couple of things to get off his chest:

HARRY You went over to 'them'.
OLIVER Yes.
HARRY You damn nearly landed us with a ministry of security running a secret police.
OLIVER I was perhaps somewhat blinded by ambition.
HARRY 'Somewhat' blinded?
OLIVER You can't force my resignation you know. This is only a one-all draw.
A beat. Then Harry calls.
HARRY James, same again for Mr Mace. I'll have a large, usual. Not on my tab.

A one-all draw indeed. We are all looking forward to the next match.

Oliver Mace is played by Tim McInnerny, best-known for his much-loved portrayal of classic upper-class twit Lord Percy Percy in *Blackadder*.
   All shades of the 'dimwit I can't seem to shake off' are gone. McInnerny's Mace is believably ruthless, patronising and supercilious. He previously worked with writer Howard Brenton on his play *Pravda*, co-written with David Hare.

SPOOKS 3.2

DIRECTOR: JONNY CAMPBELL

[Scriptwriter: Howard Brenton]

> ❝ I had no idea lying had such a complex molecular structure...Fred Roberts ❞

Once again, art mirrors life – 3.2 starting with a deliberate, MI5-engineered explosion in a block of derelict East End flats. MI5 puts it about that the blast has been caused by 'Red Mercury', a nuclear accelerant.

Red Mercury is a CIA-inspired fiction. But as we write, several men are on trial at London's Central Criminal Court accused of trying to procure it for the purposes of terrorism. You can't make it up – or can you?

In the next phase of 'Operation Flytrap', Harry Pearce reawakens Fred Roberts, the 'sleeper' scientist he recruited twenty-four years previously (*right*). Fred's Nobel prize-winning career is founded on research data supplied by MI5, and now it's payback time: Fred's job is to help ensnare an active terrorist cell which is trying to create a nuclear bomb. He must convince them he has not only manufactured Red Mercury, but needs to sell it in order to pay off his massive, MI5-created 'gambling debts'. But Fred, nearing retirement, doesn't want to repay his debt:

HARRY That was the agreement. We'd help you become an expert in your field and if we ever wanted to call on your expertise we would.
FRED What am I, Faust? Have I sold my soul to the devil for my success?
HARRY Sold your soul to your country. What's wrong with that?
FRED Go back into the woodwork, you spook.

Playing dirty, MI5 arrests and questions Fred under the Anti-terrorism Act until he gives in. With the spooks watching and the media camped outside his house, Fred tells his wife about the 'gambling habit' that has ruined them. Back in harness, despite having recently executed Hermann Joyce – and put a bullet into Harry – Tom at first seems to enjoy making Fred Roberts jump through MI5's hoops.

Fred's wife and family leave home – with a terrorist tail on their car. But Harry can't risk them in a safe house: Flytrap's success depends on the fake story looking real. Keeping watch outside the flats supposedly blown apart by Red Mercury, Zoe and Danny are themselves spotted by press photographer Will North. Immediately attracted, Zoe demands Will's film. At home with minder Tom, Fred takes to drink – and philosophy: 'You know what Nietzsche said? If you look into the abyss, the abyss will look into you.' 'Pizza?' Tom replies, 'Or lasagne?'

Winning Harry's official permission to date North, Zoe goes for it, while Danny, posing as one of the professor's students, is on hand when Aleph Command terrorist Lawrence Sayle makes contact with Fred. Playing his part brilliantly, Fred explains the East End explosion was the result of a separate terrorist group's failure to handle Red Mercury correctly. Convinced, Lawrence offers Fred $5 million for five grams of Red Mercury, delivery in three days. But threatens: 'If you are an MI5 trap, be very afraid for your family ...'

Tom now makes the worst mistake a spook can make: he starts to care.

TOM I think we need to keep Fred Roberts happy. I think we've got to move his family.
HARRY We can't do that, Tom.
TOM He'll go to pieces.
HARRY Then lie to him.

Tom lies, convincing Fred his family is in an MI5 safe house. But the crack that has opened in Tom looks to be widening by the minute. Identifying chemistry student Sayle by CCTV footage, the spooks peg him as a Syrian Secret Service agent with links to Al-Qaeda. Losing his faith in both his job and Operation Flytrap, Tom's 'We're crucifying a man here' speech leaves Zoe and Danny cold. But not as cold as Harry, when Tom tells him, 'I don't have faith in the operation.' Sending Tom home to get some sleep, Harry calls Adam in for a pointed chat.

Spiralling into breakdown, Tom tells Fred his family is not in fact safe, and that he is closing Flytrap down. With Tom and Fred Roberts now on the run and the whole operation at risk, Harry wants to pull the plug. But Adam is sure Flytrap can still pay off. In a taut sequence, a helicopter halts Tom's car.

In the stand off, everyone – even Fred Roberts – is against Tom. Flytrap must run its course. Any other move puts the professor's family in even greater danger. Faced with a broken spook, Harry decommissions Tom: 'You are no longer an officer of the Service.' Quinn's career with MI5 is over.

Roberts goes back to the lab. Arriving to collect the Red Mercury, Sayle walks straight into the MI5 flypaper – and Adam's Koranic reminder: 'It is written: as for those who have done evil, evil shall be rewarded with like evil.' In position at the Roberts family home, Special Forces cut down the terrorists who now come to take revenge.

In a sad coda to the story, Fred's 'I did it for MI5 ... I did it for the country' plea to his traumatised wife fails to pacify her. Tom fares better: escaping disciplinary action and with a generous pay off, he is now and for ever more 'James Archer'. Just another member of the great, anonymous British public.

Red Mercury features on the Internet as a real substance. This modern-day sorcerer's gold is supposedly powerful enough to trigger a fusion reaction without the need for nuclear fission. Sources differ over whether it was made up by the CIA or the KGB, but it is completely fictitious. In September 2004 three men were arrested for trying to buy a kilo for £300,000 after a 'sting' operation set up by 'Fake Sheikh' *News of the World* journalist Mazher Mahmood. The question is, can someone be imprisoned for trying to buy something that does not exist?

SPOOKS 3.3

DIRECTOR: CILLA WARE

[Scriptwriter: Rupert Walters]

'Harry, we may not be able to see the massed, red-coated ranks of England's finest piling across the field of Waterloo, but to all intents and purposes, we are at war...Oliver Mace '

We pick up the story with MI5/MI6 overseer Oliver Mace in the West Bank, horse-trading with Muhammed Khordad, leader of Pakistani terror group the Path of Light. A newly recruited British 'friend', Khordad wants to know the name of the double-agent who betrayed him in the distant past.

The real action begins in a bookshop, where famous writer Zuli is taking tea with Harakat, the shop's owner and a friend. With shades of Salman Rushdie, Zuli has a *fatwah* on his head for offending Muslim sensibilities.

Armed with a 9mm Beretta pistol, Danny – with Zoe, Colin and armed Special Branch outside in the obbo van – is on CQP [Close Quarter Protection] duty bodyguarding Zuli. But MI5's CCTV coverage is jammed. A masked gunman jumps the shop spraying bullets. Danny fires back. But the real hero is Harakat, who takes the gunman on and gets a flesh wound (*left*). The cavalry crash in – but the would-be assassin escapes.

Seeing her off to a friend's wedding on the arm of new heartthrob Will North, Danny urges Zoe to think about what she really wants. Sadly for Danny, it's not him.

Furious about the attack and the injury to Harakat, Zuli now arranges his own protection.

Adam is quick to point out the obvious: if the gunman knew when and where to strike, MI5 has a mole. Suspicious also as to why the gunman did not take the clear chance to kill Zuli when he had it, Adam asks Ruth to find out about Harakat. Ruth thinks Harakat's background – 'too real to be a real life' – smells like an MI6 legend. Adam tasks Danny to bodyguard Harakat – and worm more out of him.

Blanking Harry's suspicious prodding, Mace treats Harry's request that he run a background check on Harakat with typical disdain.

Malcolm shows Danny the jamming device that took out the CCTV signal from the bookshop just before the attack: professional kit. The kind a government agency uses.

Hunting for the likely gunman, Zoe and Ruth trawl the databases looking for a face match on the bookshop's CCTV footage. It's late-at-night Ruth who eventually finds one: but only after Malcolm has practised his joke-telling skills:

> **Doctor, doctor, I've got a cricket ball stuck up my bum.
> Howzat?
> Don't you start.**

The ID they come up with isn't pretty: hitman for hire Sharaf Al-Youm.

At the wedding, Zoe tells Will about her alternative identities and how these cover roles are fully backed up by credit cards, passports, bogus 'relatives' and all other necessary 'legendary' means. The kind of trust that puts her job on the line, its other name is love.

Zoe calls Adam to warn him Al-Youm has arrived in the UK and gone to ground in a London suburb. Still convinced Harakat is not all he seems, Adam tells Danny to take Harakat to a safe house.

Bonding over a shared obsession with cricket, Harakat makes Danny a present of a rare 1913 *Wisden*. In return, Danny offers Harakat a tour of Lord's cricket ground.

One of Harry's contacts sends him surveillance evidence of the Mace/Khordad meeting we saw at the start. Adam asks Harry if they can use the Whitehall mole to find out more. With a meeting arranged, Adam's job is to protect her. Now realising he, too, has a leak, Mace orders a team to tail Adam. Game on.

Adam gets full support in a 'category A counter-surveillance' op to make sure Harry's anonymous source stays that way. In a brilliantly engaging MI5 v MI6 duel across some of London's most scenic sites, Adam – with a little help from his friends – shows us how to play the counter-surveillance game. Using a 'chokepoint' to expose MI6 watchers, Zoe directs Adam across the Millennium Footbridge. Zoe thinks he's clear. Until Sam comes up with a numberplate match on a car that has already 'rotated' past Adam before.

The high-pace surveillance duel continues, with Adam joining a rowing team running through the City and then plunging into the Underground. In the end, it's old hand Harry who helps Adam 'clear his coat-tails', trapping Mace's watchers inside a tube train. Adam changes trains – and MI6 loses him.

Harry's mole meets Adam on Primrose Hill and tells him that the whole bookshop 'hit' was an elaborate deception to make Harakat's assassination look like a botched attempt to kill Zuli (*right*). The Path of Light's 'engineer' [bomb maker] before MI6 recruited him, Harakat is the real target. While Danny takes Harakat on a once-in-a-lifetime tour of Lord's, the mole tells Adam that Khordad and the terrorists want Harakat's head on a plate. In return the Path of Light will help protect Western interests. Hitman Al-Youm was a decoy. The real hitman is out there, waiting to strike. And the spooks have no idea who or where he is.

For all of their cleverness, they have been outflanked.

Adam's information comes too late to stop Danny and Harakat leaving Lord's, and much too late to stop the heavy-duty sniper bullet that now blasts through Danny's back window shattering Harakat's head.

Harry wants to know why Mace would conspire in the assassination of his own agent. For Mace – in a statement that sums up the overall thrust of series three – the post 9/11 realities dictate that the end justifies the means. The killing was worth it for all the lives that might be saved by the West's new-found Path of Light 'friends'. Only one real positive comes out of the case: Adam accepts Harry's invitation to stay on the MI5 strength.

After the wedding, with a blissfully happy Zoe telling jokes and Will quoting Shakespeare's 'MI5 favourite' *Sonnet 138*, they promise always to tell one another the truth. As if.

Not many television series have their own favourite sonnet, so here in all its glory is Shakespeare's *Sonnet 138*:

When my love swears that she is made of truth,
    I do believe her, though I know she lies,
That she might think me some untutor'd youth,
    Unlearned in the world's false subtleties.
Thus vainly thinking that she thinks me young,
    Although she knows my days are past the best,
Simply I credit her false-speaking tongue;
    On both sides thus is simple truth suppress'd.
But wherefore say she not she is unjust?
    And wherefore say not I that I am old?
O, love's best habit is in seeming trust,
    And age in love loves not to have years told.
Therefore I lie with her, and she with me,
    And in our faults by lies we flattered be.

SPOOKS 3.4

DIRECTOR: CILLA WARE

[Scriptwriter: Ben Richards]

❝ If there were more people like her in the world we wouldn't need so many peace conferences. Adam Carter ❞

Adam is bugging his old friend Patricia Norton as she tries to rescue a crucial round of Middle East peace talks. Art imitating real life: in the run-up to Gulf War II, MI6 bugged the UN Secretary General's office to find out who was for and against a crucial vote.

Uxorious Adam's wife Fiona appears for the first time working for MI6. But worried Norton has a warning for her two friends: fanatical Israeli group the November Committee and ruthless, virulently pro-Zionist British newspaper proprietor David Swift are bent on wrecking the talks. Norton, who should have heeded her own warning, is then abducted, making the job personal for Adam and Fiona (*right*).

Danny's undercover task as activist 'Chris' is to find out if the November Committee's opponents, the pro-Palestinian MP David Ashworth and the Palestinian Freedom Campaign [PFC], are channelling funds to terrorists. Danny films Ashworth – and Ashworth's boyfriend Richard Hollins – at a PFC meeting. The surprise on the footage comes in the shape of pro-Palestinian filmmaker Catherine, Harry Pearce's estranged daughter by his divorced wife, whose presence in the narrative mix now makes it personal for Harry, too.

With Zoe riding shotgun, Adam uses the '£50 note/checking on my unfaithful girlfriend' ruse to get past the newspaper's security guard and into Swift's office. He downloads the entire contents of Swift's computer hard drive for Malcolm to de-encrypt.

Ruth briefs the team on the David Swift/November Committee goal – a Greater Israel, with the Palestinians ethnically cleansed from the Occupied Territories. No 'Palestinian state for peace' solution of the kind Norton was trying to broker. Not at any price.

Harry – hypocritically, given his prior 'always better to keep personal feelings out of these matters' comment – asks Danny to wear a wire and talk to Catherine. And hears the last thing he wants to hear: Catherine saying, 'My father's dead, or might as well be.'

Norton turns up dead. Despite the forensics, Adam refuses to believe she shot herself under the pressure of an extra-marital affair (as is being suggested). Analysing his computer files, Ruth confirms Swift is a senior member of the November Committee. The hard drive

also holds a list of targets encoded for what is euphemistically called 'varying treatment'. 'Nablus' means blackmail. Anyone marked 'Jenin' – like Norton – is tagged for execution. Ashworth is one of the fifteen names on the Jenin list. And Swift has an agent inside the PFC offices.

Looking to use Ashworth as bait to nuke the November Committee, Adam accuses Swift to his face of conspiracy to murder: 'Shake the tree and see what flies out.' Undeterred by Harry's furious reaction, Adam orders a watch on everyone in the PFC office. Danny, arriving late at night, finds Catherine acting suspiciously.

Working as a stringer for Zoe, Will has shot official MI5 photographs of Ashworth and lover Hollins canoodling. Ashworth has been hiding the fact that he is gay, and fears it could dynamite his public image. Will asks Zoe to marry him. A blushing Zoe accepts.

Just when Will and Zoe's future is looking rosy, Will's black-sheep brother Andy turns up. He steals copies of the explosive Ashworth/Hollins photographs and tries to sell them to a national newspaper. Assuming it's Will, Ruth and Malcolm intercept them and tell Danny to give Zoe the bad news – the love of her life has betrayed her.

An intercept suggests Catherine is Swift's PFC informant.

Danny finds photographs of Catherine's Mossad ex-boyfriend. And in a top example of opportunistic double bluffing, accuses her of being an Israeli spy. In fact, Catherine is setting up a massive TV documentary exposé on Swift. Catherine ends up taking Danny to bed.

Adam suggests the 'Muhammed Ali and the rumble in the jungle strategy' – let Swift think he's won. 'We stay on the ropes and let him lead us to their agent.' For this, they need someone to plant a tracking device on Swift. 'It requires a woman who's ruthless, vicious, immoral and utterly lacking in human sympathy.' Cue his wife Fiona, the 'swallow' they will use to get up close and personal to Swift.

Swift takes Fiona's bait. Adam lets them get as far as the hotel bedroom and then extracts Fiona using a 'child with meningitis' ploy.

Danny tells Catherine his real identity – with predictable results. But the revelation has one good outcome – the partial reconciliation of Catherine and an unusually emotional Harry (*left*).

Swift's PFC insider turns out to be Richard Hollins. His sister Phoebe, we now learn, died in a Palestinian suicide bombing. Instead of going with his lover for their anniversary celebration, Hollins takes Ashworth to the PFC campaign office to kill him. A solo Zoe tries to help, but Hollins kicks the chair out from under Ashworth. Arriving in the nick of time, Danny saves the day.

Playing Swift the [brilliantly acted] CCTV footage of a battered-looking Fiona claiming he raped her, Adam gives Swift an ultimatum: 'You lose your paper. You leave the country. It's a small price to pay for the murder of a brilliant and principled woman. You bastard.'

SPOOKS 3.5

DIRECTOR: JUSTIN CHADWICK

[Scriptwriter: David Wolstencroft]

❛ It's different if you pull the trigger. **Danny Hunter** ❜

On the shooting range with Danny, Colin tells him the act of killing changes everyone: 'They've just seen a bullet that they've fired hit another living, breathing person ...I mean, once you've seen that, can you ever look at anything with the same eyes?'

Adam, Harry and Ruth get a heads up on rogue biochemist Eric Newland, suspected of developing a new version of the pneumonic plague for the North Koreans. Zoe and Danny are tasked to warn Newland off.

Sam catches Ruth red-handed in a spot of unauthorised research into John Fortescue, a City type she has come to fancy in the course of routine surveillance.

Earwigging his telephone conversation, Ruth has booked a seat in a restaurant next to him (*right*). As their hands touch over a dropped knife, Ruth learns he is going to a 'scratch Requiem' Mozart concert that night.

Ruth discovers that Newland has already been paid by the North Koreans to deliver the new plague virus.

Harry refers it upstairs and gets a coded 'papal bull' from the DG: 'We have a black flag.' Assassination.

Adam asks Zoe – seasick on the ferry tailing Newland with Danny – to open her case and take out the false bottom. A nest of hypodermic syringes stares back at her. They're not playing scarecrow any more. They are in international waters – and what started out as a low-key warning has turned into a 'clinical wet job'.

ADAM Newland is involved in the sale of weapons of mass destruction and in the light of this he has been classified as a combatant. And as a combatant, threatening UK interests, we are within our rights to take whatever actions ...we deem necessary.
ZOE Well say it. Go on, at least have the guts to say it.
HARRY We are within our rights to kill him.
ZOE We are nowhere near our rights.

Seasick and sick at heart, Zoe isn't up to the job. Danny's view is that the Increment [MI5's dedicated Special Forces unit] should do the job. But to save Zoe, he volunteers to take it on.

Back in the sub-plot, Sam and Malcolm – who will pose as her brother – have encouraged stalker Ruth to go to the Requiem and engage with the man of her dreams.

Winging back through the moral ether to an earlier David Wolstencroft episode [1.2], a hesitant Danny recalls what Tom Quinn said to 'pro-life' terrorist Mary Kane: 'Murder in the name of life is just about the stupidest thing I've ever come across.' But Adam gets him to focus and do the job.

ADAM Soon as he's under, asleep, unconscious, get on with it. Don't give yourself any time to get anxious.

Caught out by the fictitious stories he has told about having killed in the past, Danny starts to suffer massive stress, visualising himself in Newland's place. The sweet/sour counterpoint in this episode now works for us in earnest: Ruth needs Sam's help before taking the romantic plunge, while Danny needs Adam's to proceed in the small matter of extra-judicial murder. Cosying up to a sozzled Newland in the bar, Danny slips him the knock-out drops. Adam is still nursemaiding:

ADAM It only really first kicks in when you get home. First, your legs. They just go from under you. Then you puke. Then you cry like a baby... And after all that, what I finally realised was, if I could look myself in the eyes. In the mirror. If I could do that... I'd be okay.

The Ruth sub-plot pays off, allowing a deft and ironically telling intercut between high culture and base assassination. At the sticking point, Danny hesitates – then kills (*left*).

Like teenagers on a first date, Ruth and John begin clumsily: 'So what's it like doing tennis in Spain? Is it – hot?' As they start to connect, things look promising. But they miss the crucial kiss and the moment is gone.

Emotionally drained, Danny's white knight act finally cracks. He gives Zoe the disastrous news: Will's rogue brother Andy tried to sell the covert Ashworth surveillance shots from episode 3.4 as a scoop to a major newspaper. Which suggests Will has broken her trust and told Andy that she works for MI5.

In a heart-wringing scene Zoe – Keeley Hawes acting her socks off – confronts Will. 'You just destroyed everything our future was built on. Don't you ever contact me again.' Still distraught, Zoe finds the wedding florist's message on the phone and a Danny who can't comfort her. Danny doesn't do comfort any more. But he can look himself in the eyes.

SPOOKS 3.6

DIRECTOR: JUSTIN CHADWICK

[Scriptwriter: Ben Richards]

> ❝ We're denied the luxury of moral absolutes. **Danny Hunter** ❞

Faced with finding a way of letting Zoe [Keeley Hawes] leave *Spooks*, writer Ben Richards has her on trial charged with involuntary manslaughter and conspiracy to murder. Interviewed by Detective Sergeant Loughton, Zoe's 'crime' centres on the deaths of undercover Metropolitan police officer Hasan Doyan, Turkish gang boss Emré Celenk and his bodyguard Memetz Salem.

In deep cover on 'Operation Aladdin' as 'Sophie Newman', Zoe has infiltrated a Turkish mafia gang to find out if its members are running weapons to Al-Qaeda terrorists. The prosecution's key allegation is that Zoe manipulated gang lieutenant Sevilin Ozal into killing the three victims by exciting his sexual jealousy.

Chatting with Attorney-General Young, Harry protests that Zoe is being scapegoated: with an election looming, the government wants to 'brandish its liberal credentials' by throwing an MI5 case officer to the media wolves.

The Old Bailey trial stands. But Young assures Harry that even if she is found guilty, Zoe will get off with a slap on the wrist. Scared and desperate, Zoe contacts ex-fiancé Will who forgives her (*right*).

The trial of 'officer X' begins. The Crown calls Sevilin Ozal, serving seventeen life sentences for murder, who tells the court he met 'Sophie Newman' in a casino – complete with a rigged roulette wheel. Whirling us in flashback to a scene that comes straight out of James Bond, Zoe, dazzling in a designer dress, wraps Ozal round her little finger (*overleaf*).

Under Zoe's spell, Ozal takes her shopping and to dinner. Surprised in his office as she replaces a faulty bug, Zoe pretends she is there finding out about Ozal's wife. Ozal's smooth, sinister boss Emré Celenk now glides into frame.

Celenk – who clearly doesn't need it – asks Ozal's permission to take Zoe to Germany for the weekend. In another direct Bond reference, Zoe/Sophie tells Celenk she 'works for an import/export company'. On her return, Zoe goads jealous Ozal to breaking point:

ZOE You know killing me isn't going to help you. He's the one that laughs at you. Killing me is just going to make him laugh even more.

OZAL He laughs at me?

ZOE Yeah, as he undressed me.

OZAL I'm gonna kill him!

ZOE I don't think you'd dare. No I think he's more likely to have you killed. He thinks you're weak.

OZAL Weak?

ZOE Yeah, why don't you show me that you're not weak and things could be very different? Why don't you show me that you care enough about me?

In a bleak, vicious sequence Ozal shoots Celenk, his bodyguard and Doyan dead. On the wire Doyan was wearing at the time of his murder, the jurors can hear Ozal saying, 'Sophie told me what happened. She told me to kill you.' Harry turns up at Zoe's flat, to make sure she sticks to the agreed MI5 script.

The big lie Zoe repeats in court is to claim MI5 did not know undercover Met police officer Doyan was on the op. The Crown barrister spots the fact that the tapes from the new bug Zoe planted in Ozal's office – which might prove MI5 did know – are missing. Zoe claims they have been mislaid. But the Crown brief is brilliant: 'You used Ozal's sexual jealousy to turn him into your weapon, didn't you? . . . The goal of this shoddy, sordid operation was the death of Emré Celenk. That's the truth, isn't it?'

At home Zoe confesses the truth to Danny: she told Ozal to kill Celenk because she was frightened. She is to blame both for her own and for MI5's predicament.

Found guilty on all charges, Zoe gets ten years. Outraged, Harry turns the screw on the Attorney-General. Unless there is some way out for Zoe, Establishment figures will go down with her: 'We know where the bodies are buried – remember?' They reach a deal: another prisoner will get a ten-year reduction in sentence for assuming Zoe's identity. But Zoe – honourable to the end – turns the offer down. It's left to Danny to convince her to accept the 'Gina Hamilton' cover story and a new life in Chile: 'Take the passport . . . it's your freedom . . . Harry had to threaten a coup to get it.'

Zoe takes the passport. Danny agrees to talk to Will. And *Spooks* loses one of its best assets.

SPOOKS 3.7

DIRECTOR: BILL ANDERSON

[Scriptwriter: Raymond Khoury]

> ' As the walls crumble down, so the hawks will feast
> on the carcasses of the infidel. Al-Saa'iqa "

A schoolteacher with a headache takes a common painkiller and collapses, choking to death. The UK is the target of a concerted infrastructure attack by a mystery force, designed to cause panic and anarchy. MI5's task is to hunt down the person or persons responsible. And fry them.

The paracetamol pills had been laced with toxic Menazorphine. Nine people have died and there is huge panic. Adam thinks the tampering is an inside job at the Pharmavor factory where the pills are manufactured – but Colin spots that one of the factory's suppliers has no computer security. The pills have been doctored remotely, by someone who has hacked into the manufacturer's 'recipe' for the pills.

Linguist Ruth tells us that the threat messages are ostensibly from a group calling itself 'Al-Saa'iqa': 'The Thunderclap'. Raising the stakes, Al-Saa'iqa now starts undermining the banking system.

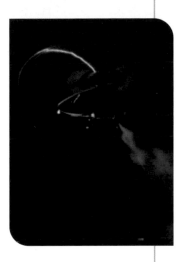

Danny is still living with the aftershock of Zoe's exile to Chile. Not to mention the 'wet job' he was obliged to carry out and the loss of his best friend and mentor Tom Quinn. Traumatised and disaffected, he stalks the Grid, in the grip of a colossal attitude problem.

Will turns up at Danny's flat, demanding to be told Zoe's whereabouts. His attempt to blackmail MI5 into telling him runs into Harry's scorn.

The attacks start a run on the Stock Exchange. But Colin's technical expertise again comes good: the routing and time delays on the threat messages allow him to pinpoint their source – a mosque. Adam and Danny race there only to find that a TV crew has also been tipped off. Fearing a set-up, Harry tells the team to stand down. But Adam goes ahead with the raid. Danny disgraces himself by needlessly assaulting a suspect. By now, the government is breathing down their necks:

GUY The PM believes this to be an act of terrorism. Which it undoubtedly is.
HARRY We'd all be on safer ground if we acted more on evidence than beliefs. Especially where others' lives are concerned, wouldn't you say?
GUY I can see you'll be at the polling station bright and early.
HARRY I mean what's next? Are muggings to be brought under this mythical 'terrorism' umbrella of yours?

Al-Saa'iqa turns the screw another notch, hacking the UK's traffic light controls and routing urgent 999 calls to a sex chatline, causing chaos, injury and death. The hackers have broken the G & J [Gibson and Joukowsky] algorithm – the 'unbreakable' [fictional] code without which nothing on the Internet is secure. The hackers want £100m. The government is prepared to pay – but only if the British get the G & J code in return.

Smart as a whip, Ruth notices that the Arabic in the hacker's messages is written by a non-native speaker. Realising the hacker loves Arabic history, poetry and literature, she has the clever idea of trawling through recent online bookstore purchase histories. She will see if she can cross-match a buyer. Things are cooking for Ruth – not least when Andrew, the hunky computer boffin she used to work with at GCHQ, is brought in to help. Hearing her plan, he invites her round to dinner.

In a moment of epiphany following their romantic exchange of Arab poetry, the truth hits Ruth: Andrew is the enemy within. She tries to make a run for it – but he grabs her.

Harry gets a real-time computer message demanding the £100m ransom be paid in diamonds. Colin tracks the message back to the source, raising hopes of an arrest – until it turns out the hacker has 'slaved' Sam's Grid computer to his. But MI5 now plays a nasty little trick of its own: Malcolm has the ransom diamonds coated with genetically modified cobra venom. Which kills on contact. The hardest thing in any blackmail plot is collecting the money – but Andrew has a brilliant solution. As Adam waits with the diamonds on the roof, a model helicopter hovers up with instructions to sling the diamonds on its hook.

Andrew, who did most of the groundbreaking work on the G & J code when the three of them were students, is bitter that Gibson & Joukowsky took the credit, money and kudos while he got nothing. He intends releasing the code so that G & J will be remembered as the guys who caused global catastrophe.

Danny, who knows Ruth can't even change her ringtone, smells a rat when a text message arrives to say she's ill. She's never ill. Harry won't take it seriously, but Danny insists. Thames House CCTV footage shows Ruth and Andrew leaving together the previous night. A quick check turns up the fact that G & J spent time at Cambridge University with Andrew. Who is dead on the floor, face down in the poisoned diamonds he extorted.

First on the scene, Danny liberates Andrew's laptop with the sole copy of the priceless G & J code on it – dumping it in the Thames to make sure the government can't grab it. And rounds off a good day's work by calling Will North.

SPOOKS 3.8

DIRECTOR: BILL ANDERSON
[Scriptwriter: Howard Brenton]

❛ The dark pit opens. Harry Pearce ❜

This time round, the team get to do 'something cuddly' – find little Alfie, the baby kidnapped right under the noses of newly knighted rock star Sir Riff – 'the jewel in the crown of British grunge' – and wife Brenda 'call me B' Rawlings (*right*). The snatch happened in the middle of the post-palace celebrations – which in B's case included large inhalations of cocaine.

Given its political sensitivity, JIC über-spook Oliver Mace – and Downing Street – want a reluctant Harry to oversee operation 'Retrieve Baby Alfie' in person. Adam, who has never handled a kidnap before, turns to Michelle Molby, editor of trashy celebrity magazine *Mega*. 'Window into Fleet Street' Molby [Arabella Weir] is worth her weight when it comes to reading the celebrity zeitgeist. She tells Adam that although Riff and B are the British public's 'mass sexual fantasy', Riff's career is on the slide. And that she has already negotiated an exclusive 'kidnap story' deal with them.

At the same time, Treasury minister John Sylvester is contemplating resignation and suicide. He calls old mate Harry for help. Set up by a woman who threatened to kiss-and-tell, Sylvester lashed out with his fists. He thinks she may be dead. Vacuuming out Sylvester's mobile, Malcolm and Colin find compromising snaps of the woman in question.

Worried that B might do something silly – and so make the government look stupid for knighting Riff – Mace insists an undercover officer he has 'borrowed' from MI6 keep an eye on B. Cue Fiona.

Fiona is keen: if she can transfer to MI5, then she, Adam and son Wes might have more of the family life Adam has been complaining they lack. Haunted by premonitions of her death in the field, Adam is dead set against it.

Confronting Sylvester with the crime scene photographs of a murdered – but so far unidentified – woman found in Kensington Gardens, Harry hands Sylvester a pen, makes him write a letter of resignation and orders him to contact the police. Sylvester has blood on his hands and Harry's not going to wipe it off for him.

But Mace has a different agenda: if baby Alfie's safe return grabs the headlines then Sylvester will resign, but not for the real reason.

He tells Sylvester: 'All that concerns me is that the government does not fall because of your disgusting little sin.' So much for morality.

Armed with Malcolm's cocaine substitute in case she gets herself in a 'situation', a ring with a secret compartment and a tower-block-sized case full of free make up, Fiona – aka Andrea Larouche – gets alongside B. She poses as a sales agent for 'Vita Nuova', the spook-friendly cosmetics firm French Intelligence uses to trawl information from ambassadors' wives and girlfriends. The real cocaine Fiona takes in with her helps. As do her shared 'Bromley girl' legend and derrière liposuction stories.

As B and Fiona bond over a line, the ransom demand arrives: £3m in a bag. Bag in last toilet of the gents at The Hole, the club where Riff [Andy Serkis, aka Gollum and Kong] started out, cloakroom ticket behind the pipe. It all happens that same night. Or Alfie arrives in the post. Bit by bit.

In the teeth of Adam's better advice, Riff wants to pay up. Spotting a logical flaw in the pick-up arrangements, Adam realises they are a blind: having pre-loosened the brickwork behind the toilet cubicle where the cash is to be left, the kidnappers mean to punch through the wall and grab it from the street. MI5 bugs the bag, hoping to track the gang and free baby Alfie.

But the kidnappers disable the tracking device with a massively powerful electro-magnet. The gang – and the money – disappear.

Comparing notes over her cocaine-induced nosebleed, Adam and Fiona realise the whole kidnap and ransom is a B-inspired publicity stunt. But then they find little Alfie buried in a shallow grave. And discover that one of the gang is Rudolf Vino Ponti, a heroin dealer with protection from within the Italian government who used to be Riff's road manager.

B finally confesses to Fiona that she set up the kidnap of her own child, who died by accident. But her biggest concern is that 'they'll still love us'.

In a gripping finale, Riff, Ponti, B and Fiona meet at The Hole. When Ponti reveals that B was behind the kidnap, Riff stabs him and B dead and then shoots himself.

A nation mourns the Riff and B 'suicide pact'. And John Sylvester resigns, believing that will be the end of it. Only Harry Pearce has other ideas: he gets Adam to hand *Mega* editor Molby Sylvester's crime file. Which, when she publishes it, will see Sylvester in prison.

SPOOKS 3.9

DIRECTOR: ALRICK RILEY

[Scriptwriter: Rupert Walters]

> Sometimes we have no choice. Sometimes we have to behave worse than them. **Adam Carter**

Routine surveillance catches ex-Special Forces mercenary Robert Morgan behaving suspiciously. He visits an ex-Cold War KGB arms cache on a disued RAF base.

Malcolm's ultrasonic scan of the cache reveals the fact that a laser target marker [LTM] is missing. Worse, it is in London – and will be used to guide a missile into an unknown City target within seventy-two hours. Adam and Danny put Morgan to the question. But Morgan knows how to play the interrogation game. The bare cell, the sleep deprivation and the bright light aren't going to be enough to make him give up the LTM's location, the target or tell them who he is working for (*right*).

Up for the MI5 Director-General's job, Harry asks Ruth to help him prepare.

Morgan tries to muddy the waters, claiming the arms cache visit was part of a 'black bag' op that he felt was UK-government led. Playing the old 'Bad cop, good cop' routine, Adam and Danny don't buy it. When the carrot of striking a deal doesn't work they turn up the heat and Adam shows his unpleasant side. He has Morgan placed in stress positions, subjects him to constant ear-splitting noise and deprives him of food and drink. Sam asks the redundant question, 'Isn't that called torture?'

Trawling Morgan's finances, Fiona, Malcolm and Colin find out that on the same day Anglo–West African Oil sent Morgan to a bank in Saffron Walden, a private City bank paid £100,000 to an account held there in the name of Ken Johnston – one of Morgan's cover names. Time to get sneaky. Anglo–West African finance manager Juliet Taylor has made three claims on her car insurance in the preceding year. She's not going to want another one. So Fiona 'accidentally' backs into her and then offers to pay for the damage in cash. And lies further that she can help Juliet get her daughter into an exclusive school.

In a surprise development, Adam explains why we are seeing a ruthless new side to his character: he was tortured on a job in Syria for MI6 and is prepared to use the experience – if he must – to break Morgan.

Failing to break Morgan with the promise of personal bankruptcy, zero chance of future employment and the end of all life as he knows it, Adam pins Morgan in a vicious arm lock. To no effect.

Like Danny, Fiona questions Adam's use of torture – only to have him deny they've even gone that far yet. Then Ruth discovers tough guy Morgan's Achilles heel: his daughter, Mary, needs a liver transplant. With none of Danny's moral qualms, it's only a question of how Adam and Harry will use this weak spot to make Morgan talk. They might, for example, take eight-year-old Mary off the donor list. Something Adam now makes clear to their prisoner.

With time running out, Fiona goes for the throat: either Juliet finds out who in the oil company is employing Morgan – and why – or Juliet's husband finds out about her extra-marital affair. Juliet's information puts the puzzle together: to stop them getting a massive African pipeline contract, Anglo–West African intend putting a missile into the London HQ of a rival oil company. Now that's what you call corporate competition.

Out on the Thames mud, Adam shows Morgan his daughter, who is up with Danny on the balcony of the targeted building (*previous page*). If the missile comes in, Mary dies with it. Morgan breaks, revealing the whereabouts of the LTM and the team controlling it.

Harry has his DG interview. Which bears exactly on the issue this episode has been testing: in a democracy, where is the line drawn when it comes to protecting the state? Who decides it? Danny certainly feels that using an eight-year-old girl is morally unjustified. Does the end always – or ever – justify the means?

Anglo–West African bites the corporate dust. And Harry has the last word: 'You see, wrongs righted, evil-doers brought to heel, miracles performed: is there no end to our goodness, Ruth?'

He doesn't get the job.

THE REAL-WORLD MURK BEHIND THE SPIES

Section B's dilemma here is not just about torture. It is also about the very nature of Morgan's mission. It may seem incredible, but so-called 'black ops' go on under our democratic noses all the time. Here is part of a 1989 parliamentary debate, as documented in Hansard: 'There are two types of agent. There are above-the-line agents, who, in the event of an operation being compromised, cannot be denied because they are known to exist and Ministers must ultimately take responsibility for their existence if an operation is botched, there is a row and the security services' involvement is clear. There are also below-the-line agents who are deniable under all circumstances. They are buried beyond reach of the theoretical knowledge of Ministers and people like them.'

Our sources tell us that governments are using 'deniables' more and more as the 'war against terror' becomes ever more urgent. UK Security Service budgets – 'the vote' as it is mysteriously called – have nearly doubled since 9/11. (Not including the extra £85m split over three years to fund the next phase of expansion.)

The word is that the amount spent on 'consultants' has gone through the roof: immediately after 9/11, MI5 and 6 were granted £20m in 'emergency' cash.

SPOOKS 3.10

DIRECTOR: ALRICK RILEY

[Scriptwriter: Ben Richards]

' When your son is older, he'll be able to watch videos
of you burning on the Internet. **Terrorist leader Ahmed** '

There's always a bit of extra anticipation about watching the last
episode of a series: it's the best time to quit the show, which means
there is every chance one of the cast will die.

Fiona has a birthday coming up. Which prompts single man Harry
to suggest chocolates as a suitable gift. Adam knows better. He spends
months sourcing the perfect brooch from the covered Damascus souk
where he and Fiona first met.

Unmasking MI5 double-agent 'Butterfly' who has been spying in their
midst, the terrorists discover that Danny and Fiona have a meet set up
with him. Shooting Butterfly dead, they ambush the spooks and take
them hostage (*overleaf*).

Terrorist leader Ahmed gets a few things off his chest:

AHMED Have you been watching the news recently? Hospital wards filled
with burned children, your soldiers smashing into houses humiliating
my people, thousands of my countrymen tortured and killed. You have
brought chaos and anarchy to Iraq. Today we will hold you to account.
FIONA We?
AHMED It is you who decided that the war on terror involved invading
my country. OK, so we are all Al-Qaeda now.

With a knife at Danny's throat, Fiona is forced to read out a statement
admitting she is a British spy, and Ahmed delivers his ultimatum: either
the UK government announces the immediate withdrawal of all British
forces from Iraq, or he burns Fiona and Danny to death.

Luckily, Special Branch have sent over some extra help in the
handsome shape of Zafar Younis (Raza Jaffrey): 'I'm exploring my
identity crisis: British or Asian, Asian or British – it's tearing me apart.'

Faced with a choice between saving her son's life – they know where
his school is – or luring her husband into a trap, Fiona chooses Wes.
Their birthday 'lunch date' arranged on the phone leaves a shocked
Adam at the tender mercies of female terrorist Khatera. Fiona tries to
warn Adam about Butterfly – and gets pistol-whipped for her trouble.

Aware the terrorists will kill Fiona and Danny if he raises the alarm,

and insisting it will get noticed if he doesn't call in for a routine status report, Adam tells Ruth he bought Fiona the chocolates as she suggested. Ruth remembers she didn't: Harry did.

Ruth lays her job on the line to convince Harry something's seriously wrong. Checking the South Bank CCTV footage brings up Adam with Khatera, and that means Ruth was right: he's in big trouble. Posing as a charity collector, Zaf does a great job of slipping Adam a comms set. Harry's first resort – to have Khatera arrested – is a non-starter. She has an alarm that will trigger Fiona and Danny's execution if she's threatened – or doesn't check in with Ahmed at pre-arranged intervals.

Picking the lock of her cuffs with the birthday brooch, Fiona feigns sickness and lures in one of the guards. They kill him and escape. Danny tells Ruth to trace the mobile he's using and then chucks it. But they are recaptured. Khatera and Adam wait in a seedy hotel.

Security & Intelligence Co-ordinator Guy Facer tells Harry what he already knows – under no circumstances will the Prime Minister announce the withdrawal of British troops from Iraq – least of all at that evening's Mansion House dinner.

Since Danny killed one of the guards in the escape attempt, Khatera relays the choice Adam now has to make. To settle the score, either Danny or Fiona must die. As Adam hesitates, Danny, demonstrating the kind of bravery we would all like to think we have, taunts Ahmed into shooting him: 'Fuck you, you death-worshipping fascist.' One screaming, dreadful, heart-stopping moment later and the deed is done: Ahmed puts a bullet into Danny's brain. And a true *Spooks* hero lies dead.

Showing her the tracking device concealed in the sweet Zafar passed to him on the South Bank, Adam convinces Khatera MI5 knows where they are. But she makes Adam talk them in through the Mansion House security cordon. Back on the Grid, Zaf calls it right: the terrorists always knew there would be a 'no deal' response to their Iraq ultimatum. It was a double bluff. The real threat is to the Prime Minister and his Western-friendly dinner guests. Khatera is a human bomb, with enough explosives inside her gut to detonate the nerve gas in there with it and kill everyone in the room. Ahmed, waiting on the signal from the device concealed in Khatera's lipstick, remotely controls the detonator packaged inside her.

But Adam convinces a trembling Khatera to pass him the lipstick and raises the alarm. The PM is safe. But Fiona isn't. Realising there is something wrong when there's no trigger signal, Ahmed douses her in petrol. In a nail-biting climax, a Special Forces sniper shoots dead the terrorist on the point of setting Fiona ablaze. As Ahmed takes aim at her, a second SF soldier takes the shot that puts paid to one of MI5's worst-ever enemies.

Fiona and Adam are reunited, but it's a Pyrrhic victory: Danny has left *Spooks* for good. Feet first.

SPOOKS 4.1

DIRECTOR: ANTONIA BIRD
[Scriptwriter: Ben Richards]

❝ We are a stain on the planet. Michael Monro ❞

It's bad enough having to bury Danny. But terrorism, especially the kind of boutique terrorism the West increasingly has to confront, now makes things a whole lot worse. There's no time to grieve for a lost comrade. A massive bomb explodes in central London, killing nine women and children. Fifty more are expected to die. It was planted by nihilist eco-terrorist group 'Shining Dawn'.

Shining Dawn spokeswoman Lydia warns that unless Michael Munro, the group's leader, is released from a British prison and escapes deportation to the USA, it will detonate one bomb every ten hours: 'Be warned that our aim will be maximum civilian casualties.' With only nine hours left to catch the bombers 'Gold Commander' Harry needs all the help he can get – except possibly the enforced assistance of CIA experts Richard Boyd, Jim O'Shea and Patrick Clacey. With a wave of US bombings behind them, they are still throwing the Agency's weight about.

Shining Dawn believes that:

MUNRO We're about to be enslaved by technology and genetic engineering. We matter only insofar as we consume. We will destroy [the planet], along with all the species that inhabit it, unless humans are dramatically culled.

CIA expert Boyd says that catching the group's bomb-maker is the key to defeating the crackpot group.

Ruth is detailed to quiz Shining Dawn 'guru' Professor Stephen Curtis in Oxfordshire about his contacts with the group. Harry now gets yet more unsolicited help in the form of the hyper-ambitious Juliet Shaw, brushing up her operational skills before the interview for National Security Co-ordinator. CCTV footage and a chance road accident lead Adam, Zaf and Juliet to Carl Mortimer, a utilities company manager who hired the van used in the first bombing.

The married Mortimer loaned his credit card to 'Delphine', a French girlfriend he met only in hotels. She told him she used it to help immigrants. Threatening him with Abu Ghraib and Guantanamo Bay, Adam and Zaf take Mortimer outside. Where a sniper shoots him through the head. The fact that someone knew about their meeting

with Mortimer means there is a mole somewhere in the loop. Harry gets the Home Secretary's promise of full support when MI5 catches the traitor.

As Ruth interrogates the sneering Curtis, terrorist gunman Joe Kennedy – who has already shot dead her Special Branch escort – comes to kill him. With no mobile phone signal and no car, they run for it.

Posing as workers, the cell plants a bomb at a London railway station. But not before waitress Tash [Martine McCutcheon, *below*] collides with bomb-maker Owen Forster, and takes a long, hard look at his face when he fails to apologise.

Adam, Zaf and Harry listen in as Juliet Shaw gets Carl Mortimer's widow to tell her he regularly met Delphine at the Marcelline Hotel, Belgravia. The Marcelline's CCTV footage helps identify known Shining Dawn activist and French citizen Jeanette Sechard, aka 'Lapin'.

Spouting Homer and refusing to co-operate, Curtis reckons without Ruth's encyclopedic knowledge. She works out that Curtis met Munro at an address that includes the name 'Achilles'.

Crosschecking against the 'Lapin' alias, Colin locates Jeanette, who seems forewarned, chucking her SIM card away and bolting even as Special Branch come for her. Cornered, she refuses to drop her bag, which the police have to assume contains a weapon, and she's shot. Luckily the activist's SIM card indicates the location of the next bomb – a mainline London railway station – but it still seems the mole has been busy again. And must be someone very senior. Suspicion turns to Juliet.

As the station is evacuated, the police start ushering everyone back in. Shining Dawn has warned of a second bomb in the street outside. Super-cool Adam points out the group doesn't give warnings – its entire purpose is to cause as many deaths as possible. He countermands the order and evacuates the station. The team have stopped the second bombing just in time – but the clock is already ticking on the third device.

Having had an affair with the married Harry while they worked together in the 1970s on Operation Omega, Juliet Shaw now uses her knowledge of his past mistakes to try to blackmail him.

Spotting Forster on the first station's CCTV – and realising that waitress Tash might be able to identify him – Adam and Zaf go to bring her in. Zaf heads off en route to check out a Special Branch tip-off about suspect activity at a warehouse. Heading for Thames House with Tash, Adam suspects Zaf may be in trouble. Alerted by Zaf's mobile phone, Shining Dawn men Neil and Peter have grabbed Zaf, beaten him up and tied him to a chair. They believe Zaf is Adam Carter – marked for assassination, like key witness Tash.

Which is where we leave this episode – on the cliff-face with Adam, Tash and Zaf clinging on by their fingernails.

SPOOKS 4.2

DIRECTOR: ANTONIA BIRD

[Scriptwriter: Ben Richards]

> The one thing my humanity has given me is an awareness of the nightmare my species has become. **Richard Boyd**

We left Zaf at the end of episode 4.1 with Shining Dawn terrorists Neil and Peter about to shoot him(*right*). Something Adam, having just been to Danny's funeral, will do anything to prevent. Rummaging up a container of white spirit he uses this and the vodka mixers Tash – like all good south London girls – keeps in her handbag to improvise a brace of Molotov cocktails.

With persuaded bravery, Tash draws the terrorists away from Zaf, giving Adam the chance to detonate the Molotovs. A short, vicious scrap ends when Adam shoots Peter in the leg. Tash, helping Zaf get free, fights with the best of them.

Adam catches up with the crawling terrorist and tries to make him reveal where the next bomb is hidden. When Peter fails to talk, Adam drags him to the fire escape, dangles him out over the railing and asks him again. Lashing out with his feet, Peter slips, smacking into the concrete below at terminal velocity. Did he fall, or was he dropped?

Now it's Neil's turn. Wisely, he decides to talk. But he knows only that the bomb is in a block of flats 'somewhere in east London'.

Haunted as always by his past, Harry comes clean rather than give in to Juliet's threats and offers the Home Secretary his resignation. As we began to discover in episode 4.1, back in the Cold War Harry helped run Operation Omega, staging outrages to stir the anti-Communist pot. Mistakenly trusting a rogue agent, he caused unnecessary deaths. The Home Secretary asks Harry to wait until the emergency is over.

Using the information Adam extracted from Neil, the police find the third device at the base of a tower block, evacuate the residents and defuse the bomb with less than five minutes left on the clock.

Malcolm encourages Tash to make a photofit image of the terrorist she bumped into at the station. The spooks are closing in. But will the mole let them?

Still babysitting arrogant Professor Curtis, Ruth gets the minders to stop him wandering away. Only to look up and see Joe Kennedy coming at Curtis with a knife (*overleaf*). Opening fire on Adam and Zaf, Kennedy escapes.

With its firing sequence encoded and the code known only to Owen Forster, no one will be able to defuse Shining Dawn's next bomb. It has what Forster calls 'a nice little surprise' attached to it.

Colin's way of flirting with Tash is to show her the latest spook technology – a tiny tracking/listening device that prints the speaker's words onto a remote screen.

Harry and Adam think they've worked it out. Using the Level 1 clearance she demanded, Juliet lured Adam to the warehouse: she's the mole. Toying with them, Juliet admits it. And then hits them with the reality: not only has she identified the bomb-maker as Owen Forster by doing the hard photo-matching yards herself, she has also cracked the case. The interrogating officer who recommended Forster's release just before the group's US bombing campaign was none other than CIA man Richard Boyd. The real mole.

Boyd, who wanted Curtis dead to cover his own tracks, instead fatally shoots henchman Kennedy for failing to kill the professor. Still very much alive in the supposed safety of Thames House, Curtis recognises Boyd. Realising he's blown, Boyd drops his Thames House security badge into a passing spook's pocket as a decoy.

Posing as her driver, Boyd takes Tash hostage. But feisty Tash activates Colin's patent voice tracker so the spooks know Boyd has her, whacks him in the soft parts and makes a run for it. Boyd catches up with her and makes it down to the basement. Following a short game of hide-and-seek, Zaf and Adam arrest him. But Boyd has already told Forster that Tash has identified him – making her the next target for assassination. Shining Dawn shoot her single police escort dead leaving Tash once again a hostage.

A new posse of CIA men are in town, at Harry and the Home Secretary's behest. Boyd goes under the bright lights:

ADAM I'm assuming you can still contact Owen Forster?
BOYD nods.
ADAM You'll call him and say that you have to meet him face to face.
BOYD Oh yeah – and why would I do that?
ALEX Because you know what happens to a man when he has his eyelids taped open and he's kept awake for a month?

Boyd cuts a deal. Luring Forster to a meeting, he gets the bomb-maker to tell him the latest bomb is at the back of the Royal Eastern General Hospital. With Special Forces ready in position to kill Forster if need be, a CIA hit man shoots Boyd dead instead. They want this embarrassment out of the way. Forster tries to run for it, but SF arrest him.

Knowing the bomb's location isn't enough: without the trigger code, all MI5 can do is evacuate the building. Leaving Forster's 'little surprise' – Tash – hardwired to the explosives.

With the bomb clock ticking down through thirteen minutes, Professor Curtis – facing up to the error of his ways – fences with Forster to crack the code:

CURTIS Munro was Typhon and you'd have used the handle ... Kronos. Am I correct?
JULIET Who's Kronos?
CURTIS Son of Gaia, the earth mother. He violently defended his mother by cutting off the genitals from her assailant. Shining Dawn believe that they are agents for the spirit of Gaia.

The clock is ticking. With the hospital evacuated, Adam disobeys Harry's direct order that he leave Tash to die alone. But his last-ditch attempt to disconnect Tash from the bomb makes the timer run down faster, leaving him no choice but to reconnect her. Curtis works out Owen's terrorist codename – Kronos 2 – and Adam stops the bomb clock with seconds to spare.

Harry gets to be a hero, not a resignation case. Zaf's sterling work sees him offered a permanent job with MI5. As for the egregious Juliet Shaw:

HOME SECRETARY The Prime Minister is minded to make Juliet the new national security co-ordinator.
A beat.
HOME SECRETARY Do you have a view on that?
HARRY She's a ruthless, untrustworthy, right-wing crazy who'll stop at nothing.
HOME SECRETARY Hmmm, I got that impression. Rather a terrifying stare, also.
HARRY Hmm, that can be quite useful sometimes. I would have no objections to the appointment.

Executive Producer Jane Featherstone decided to vary the overall pace of the series, now into its fourth run, by commissioning a 'clock-ticking' thriller over two parts.

The theme was inspired by writer Ben Richards' fascination with the fact that bomb-making technology is so easily accessible. 'It means that a few crackpots can hold us all to ransom.' How right he was, given the terrible sequence of events on 7/7.

Richards lived in South America for much of his childhood, and the group's name is very like the name of the real-life 'Shining Path' Peruvian guerrilla movement. Production company Kudos had to check that there wasn't a real 'Shining Dawn'.

SPOOKS 4.3

DIRECTOR: ALRICK RILEY

[Scriptwriter: Ben Richards]

> ' I'm not like you. I have beliefs. I don't do deals...'
> **Extreme right-wing leader Keith Moran.**

Harry's 'Get me Tomahawk on a secure line' means trouble, in the shape of resurgent extreme right-wing party 'The British Way', which has several councillors and its first potential MP, William Sampson [Rupert Graves]. Cashing in on a wave of anger about asylum and immigration, Sampson has quit the Conservative party and means to stand as an independent.

With Adam undercover among the mobs attacking and evicting ethnic families, Harry is already getting it in the neck from newly promoted National Security Co-ordinator and ex-lover Juliet Shaw. The government wants MI5 to stop Sampson – by all necessary means.

Infiltrating the movement as disaffected, far-right ex-con Luke Chivers, Adam's plan is to 'make The British Way eat itself' by sowing dissent and disagreement from within. First priority is to mislead and manipulate organiser and psychopath Keith Moran. In the second prong of the attack, Fiona's mission as undercover, British Way-friendly corporate lobbyist Emily Glover is to subvert and undermine Sampson. She'll be aided in her task by Conservative MP Peregrine Howell-Davis. H-D has some sexual peccadilloes and Harry blackmails him into joining The British Way under a false flag.

Crossbow-loving Moran takes Adam birdwatching so that his men can search Adam's flat for signs he is not who he says he is. The cover holds up. Adam reports through MI5 asset 'Isis', aka MI5 link woman 'Auntie May'. She signals she is home with a vase of red plastic tulips, and passes Adam's field reports on to Zaf, also in cover as a Royal Mail postman, by means of matching high-tech pens.

Warning Moran the party is shaping to purge him, and that Sampson is behind it, Adam starts sowing the seeds of The British Way's destruction. Juliet has more direct ideas: like assassinating Sampson. An idea Harry finds utterly foolish.

Dangling a £500,000 campaign donation under Sampson's nose, Fiona attaches a few strings – like having Moran and his men expelled from The British Way and appointing Howell-Davis as his number two. In counterpoint, Zaf leads a campaign of dirty tricks designed to keep Sampson on the hop, like repainting the MP's front door and then accusing him of being in breach of local council planning regulations.

Enter Ruth, in cover as Adam's cousin and GCHQ worker Lesley. Over a set of concocted 'family' photos, Ruth passes transcripts of the conversation between Fiona, Howell-Davis and Sampson plotting 'inbred' Moran's expulsion. Going for broke, Adam encourages Moran to stage a putsch of his own and take control of The British Way.

When an Afghan asylum seeker hits the news with the murder of four-year-old white schoolgirl Melanie Roberts, a livid Moran takes Adam 'hunting' in Southall with his crossbow. Adam's dilemma: how to save the Asian child but still keep his credibility intact. He grabs the crossbow and shoots the child's father in the leg.

Keeping up the dirty tricks campaign, MI5 turns off Sampson's mains water, so that he arrives at the big press conference smelly and dishevelled. But the real damage is done when the ten MPs who were supposed to be rallying to Sampson's flag fail to turn up. Describing Sampson as a delusional liar, MI5 stooge Peregrine-Howell turns the whole thing into a farce. A triumph for the spooks.

The other jaw of the trap closes on Sampson when Moran jumps him at a British Way meeting. Warning that the general mayhem has been engineered by Adam and MI5, Sampson tries to patch things up. Moran rebuffs him – but sends his boys round to ask 'Aunty May' a few questions, following which they drown her in the bath. Worried, Ruth calls Adam who tells her to wait until he arrives. Instead, Ruth wanders into the house. Where she is grabbed by Moran's killers, who then also take Adam.

Dumped in the middle of Moran's favourite nature reserve, Ruth and Adam now become game for his crossbow (*right*). Telling Ruth to run for it, unarmed Adam charges Moran as he is reloading, but ends up looking down the wrong end of the bow. Both men have forgotten Ruth – who creeps up behind Moran and whacks him on the head.

Sampson loses the election – and Moran goes to prison for murder.

REAL UNDERCOVER WORK

In 2004, film-maker Jason Gwynne went undercover for six months with the British National Party. What he revealed falls into a rigorous journalistic category. It's called 'You just couldn't make it up'.

A ruthless new moderniser deposing the party founder, infighting, resignations, humiliations, out-of-court settlements. Perhaps an 'Adam' figure really was there in the party, spreading disinformation and rebellion. In any case, leader Nick Griffin and member Mark Collett were taken to court for 'incitement to racial hatred' after the documentary was aired on the BBC. Former party leader John Tyndall was also due to appear in court, but had died three days earlier.

Spooks's probing, in September 2005, was more than timely [it has more than once questioned not just the BNP but the political climate that allows it to flourish]. In 2006, polls found that the BNP's policies were gaining ground.

The British public didn't want to be associated with racism per se, but there were huge concerns about levels of immigration and what that means in practical terms for society, with issues like housing, education and the NHS to the fore. A year later, in the May 2006 local council elections, the BNP more than doubled its number of seats.

There may be those who think the idea of the crazed figure of Moran [played with great subtlety here by David Threlfall] is larger than life. But BNP founder John Tyndall was once 'deputy commander' of a private army called Spearhead, based on the SA of Nazi Germany. The SA, or Sturmabteilung, were Hitler's shock troops. In 1962, Tyndall was jailed for six months for training neo-Nazis. In total, this ordinary-looking, white, middle-class man with rather bad teeth was imprisoned three times.

SPOOKS 4.4

DIRECTOR: ALRICK RILEY

[Scriptwriter: Howard Brenton]

> ❛ Why are there so many people like you? Why are you crammed into a crate like this, dreaming of...what? Prostitutes on London streets? Whisky bars? How will you be cured of this poison? **Ali Mohamed Yazdi** ❜

MI6's man in Istanbul warns MI5 that a dangerous terrorist, Yazdi, is heading for Britain. He is using an illegal immigrant network operated by the playboy son of the Brit-friendly, Harrier-buying king of Bahar, Prince Hakim, who is also known as the 'Prince Who Eats Diamonds'. Is Hakim the real architect of Yazdi's planned attack on parliament?

RUTH Prince Hakim is notorious for mixing ground diamonds into his food.
ZAF Why does he do that?
RUTH To increase his potency.
ZAF moves closer to RUTH.
ZAF Does it work?
RUTH I really wouldn't like to know.

The ruthless and capable Yazdi, a founder member of terrorist group 'Al- Khaf' ['The Cave'] is on the move. Yazdi's CV includes the killing of eleven Moroccan children, at least four Israeli citizens and assorted other atrocities.

With Zaf shown the door when he tries to quiz Hakim, the spooks set up a 'rat trap', bugging Hakim's suite and filming him having sex with a female 'swallow'. Hakim then admits controlling the illegal immigration route, but flatly denies abetting Yazdi. Cue Arabic-speaking Adam's undercover mission to 'turn' Yazdi, posing as a 'Circassian construction engineer from Aleppo' equipped with a GPS tracking device and concealed comms.

'It's like pulling petals off a flower. Who's going to get killed first? You? Me?' Fiona is tortured by insecurity, and who could blame her? Adam, who is always keen to go undercover, despite Fiona's protestations, joins the illegal immigration trail in Istanbul. Yazdi also joins the truck. He takes the initiative, subjecting Adam to a quietly expert grilling.

Unable to get past Yazdi's contempt, Adam calls in the prearranged

'Dead End' callsign. It's the trigger for bogus Bulgarian bandits – in reality a team led by Zaf – to ambush the truck, forcing Yazdi and Adam to run. Adam is honest with him and offers a two-year, fixed-term double-agent deal. Which – astonishingly – Yazdi takes.

Appointed Yazdi's quizzer, Fiona extracts some alarming news: an imminent riverborne Al-Khaf attack on the House of Commons. Yazdi also gives up details of Al-Khaf London contact Hussein Hadrami, who is promptly arrested.

If you were beginning to think this all looked a mite too pat, you were right. Despite the attack warning, the Prime Minister refuses to close the House of Commons. With MI5 unable to break Hadrami, National Security Co-ordinator Juliet Shaw insists Yazdi take over the interrogation – in breach of all security protocols and Harry's express wish. Yazdi gets Hadrami to say on the record that Prince Hakim controls both the Al-Khaf London cell and the upcoming attack. But the prince angrily maintains his innocence. Both Harry and Adam are afraid Hadrami might be just a bit player and Hakim is telling the truth. Juliet overrules Harry for the second time to insist Yazdi interrogate Hakim face to face.

Juliet has walked her two-inch stilettos into a trap. Before Adam can stop him, Yazdi picks up Prince Hakim's glasses and stabs him to death. The spooks have been brilliantly duped: Yazdi's mission from the outset was to assassinate Hakim. But then, nobody wins every time out, not even MI5.

An undercover Adam with Yazdi on the illegal immigration trail.

SPOOKS 4.5

DIRECTOR: JEREMY LOVERING

[Scriptwriter: Raymond Khoury]

> ❝ Two men...against a new world order? Bringing down communism was child's play compared to fighting this velvet fascism. No, I know when to fold. **Clive McTaggart** ❞

We're back in rich series four 'how far do we go to protect the state?' territory, and picking up the 'explosive memoirs' theme touched on once before in episode 1.5. Are the security services justified in murdering a former MI5 man in order to prevent him revealing secrets that might embarrass both the state and serving officers? Discuss...

Blackmailed into handing over the manuscript of his memoirs, retired senior spook and Harry's former colleague Clive McTaggart is taken into his idyllic cottage garden and suffocated by two men. They rig the scene to make his death look like suicide. Surprising the killers in the act, Ruth's tabloid newspaper contact Gary Hicks manages to escape – and tell her the tale.

Harry and senior colleagues are reminiscing about their friend and colleague McTaggart. Harry is questioning how McTaggart's morale had fallen this low: are the security services losing their moral compass?

With the spooks busy assessing the CVs of potential MI5 recruits, Ruth rings Harry and awkwardly asks him to 'come over'. He realises Ruth's speaking in code. A talk with the chain-smoking Hicks (*right*) soon reveals that McTaggart had written a book exposing some of the morally reprehensible things going on in the spy world. The hack's presence in Ruth's flat puts her in huge danger: a team of assassins outside has a sniper rifle trained on Hicks's head. But why do they hesitate to shoot?

Roy Woodring – the same Military Intelligence spook we've just met reminiscing with Harry and Juliet over 'McTaggart's finest hour' – is listening in. Identifying Harry's voice, Woodring orders the hit team to stand down.

Harry rightly suspects a plot. Colin comes up with a lead – a woman unknown to Hicks named Jo Portman has tried repeatedly to contact him by phone and has been looking up Hicks on the internet.

Posing as gas company employee 'Roger Thornhill' [Cary Grant's character in Hitchcock's *North by Northwest*], Adam pays Portman a visit. Only to discover aspiring journalist Portman was trying to contact Hicks for a job. But nobody's fool Jo detects there is more to the dishy 'Roger Thornhill'.

Snooping at McTaggart's cottage, Adam and Fiona find signs of fibre-optic surveillance. Tired of being in spook quarantine for his own protection, Hicks – determined to write up the McTaggart story – jumps out of Zaf's car and runs into his newspaper's offices.

As Adam takes Hicks back in, a passing Jo spots them – and follows them to the MI5 safe house. Bracing him up in a nearby café, Jo demands to know who and what he really is. Adam claims he is bodyguarding Hicks, who has dug up some sensitive dirt on a VIP.

Sensing a story, Jo hangs around the MI5 safe house. She sees Ruth arrive. Ruth has no idea someone inside Thames House has planted a tracking device in her coat. A newshound to his bones, Hicks takes Ruth's phone and calls his newspaper with a view to filing the McTaggart story. Prompting Woodring to order his immediate assassination.

Watching as the thugs go in for the kill, Jo smashes a couple of car windows. Their screaming alarms alert Zaf, Ruth, Hicks and bodyguard Carl, who is wounded along with one of Woodring's killers in the epic slo-mo gunfight that now ensues.

Adam arrives to find that clever, resourceful Jo has not only saved the lives of everyone inside the safe house, but also chucked her mobile in the killers' car, enabling Malcolm to track the mobile and identify the caller as Woodring.

Far from showing any signs of conscience, Woodring justifies his former colleague's horrible murder, arguing that McTaggart's memoirs represented a 'clear and present danger' to the strength of the intelligence services. What's more, he demands Harry give up scribbler Hicks for the same treatment. Harry's having none of it. 'So where does it stop? Clive? Hicks? My people? My team? Good God, Roy. What did Clive have on you that made you completely lose your mind?'

Leaving Harry with a problem. Taking McTaggart's suicide note Malcolm and Colin create a bogus handwritten 'copy' of the memoirs. With this Harry can leverage Woodring and his pals into submission. Always provided Woodring doesn't have Harry killed first.

But is Juliet Shaw part of the conspiracy of shame? At a favourite *Spooks* location – the dolphin pillars on the Thames Embankment – Harry gets Juliet to admit she was (*left, bottom*). She claims not to have known how far Woodring would go. Harry, armed with the 'memoirs', lays it on the line. Woodring gets 'put under a rock', they call the dogs off Hicks on condition he bury the story, and Juliet reflects on her ethics, sharpish – or he releases the manuscript.

Asked to choose a new recruit from the short-list, Adam goes out and hires the remarkable Jo Portman (*left, top*).

The last irony? Harry opens his post to find a copy of the real memoirs in his hand. McTaggart's final insurance scheme.

SPOOKS 4.6

DIRECTOR: JEREMY LOVERING

[Scriptwriter: David Farr]

' It amazes me what some people will do to get a promotion.
Harry Pearce '

The spooks save a falsely imprisoned man who is blackmailed into
attempted murder.

A tip-off from French intelligence: Nazim Malek is co-ordinating
a new terror attack on London – from the British prison cell where
he has been detained without trial for two years. Harry puts pressure
on National Security Co-ordinator Juliet Shaw to have Malek released.
The hope is he will lead MI5 to the rest of the terrorist group.

No one is more pleased to see Malek go free than human rights
lawyer Rebecca Sinclair. A leading light with pro-rights outfit
'Liberation', Sinclair hires PR expert Sarah Morris to help capitalise
on Malek's release, not realising that 'Sarah Morris' is Fiona Carter
operating undercover.

The team, of course, has the Liberation offices under surveillance.
The footage shows ex-Algerian army marksman Malek behaving
strangely. He lies motionless for hours, doesn't sleep, doesn't eat.
When Fiona arrives to generate publicity for his cause, he will not
speak to her. Rebecca Sinclair arouses the watching spooks' suspicions
by leaving Malek an envelope – which he opens only after Fiona has left.

Special Branch Chief Paul Seymour arrives on the Grid, warning that
Malek is best kept locked up. This signals the start of a second plot
strand. Seymour was promoted on the strength of having caught and
imprisoned Malek, who was convicted of planning an attack on
Heathrow. But how safe was the original evidence?

When the DGSE – MI5's French counterpart – warns that mobile
phone traffic suggests an attack on – or via – the Channel tunnel, Juliet
gives Harry an ultimatum – get something on Malek that sticks, or he
goes back inside.

In a neat ironic counterpoint, a big split-screen sequence follows
Rebecca as she delivers a ringing 'human rights post 9/11' speech.

Malek suddenly makes his move. Only for Zaf to go and lose him
in the ferociously confusing Marble Arch underpasses. Adam spots
Malek on the traffic island passing 'Free Islam' extremist Rachid Medi a
rucksack. Zaf and Adam follow Rachid to a den where they find evidence
he has been forging passports – with help from Rebecca Sinclair.

It looks as if an attack is imminent. Would Rebecca or Liberation play any part in it? Rachid's brother Khaled Medi did prison time with Malek.

With the plot thickening nicely, Ruth gets shocking news: French police have just shot dead the real Nazim Malek. This can only mean that Paul Seymour arrested someone who just happened to have the same name. The real Malek has been free to carry on causing mayhem – and an innocent man was consigned to two years in a maximum-security prison.

With Harry at his throat, Paul Seymour fights back: if he's so innocent, then why is Malek trading false passports with terrorist suspects? Juliet backs Paul up – even if he was innocent of the original crime, an embittered 'Malek' is a danger to society. Adam agrees.

It's clear Rachid has some kind of hold over Malek. He wants him to carry out an assassination in return for a set of false passports. To avoid this, Malek considers jumping to his death from a tall building – and is stopped only at the last second by Zaf.

Adam and Zaf tell Malek they know he's innocent (*left*). They ask about the maps of Heathrow and British cities Special Branch found in his flat when he was arrested. Ordered in his home country to kill an entire communist village, Malek refused. He would not kill women and children. The Algerian authorities threatened to kill him, so he deserted. The circled areas on the maps were simply places he'd been hoping to live in the UK. He had told Special Branch all this at the time, but the ambitious Paul Seymour had buried it to get a clean arrest.

Adam gets the real truth from Malek: his secret is his 'illegal' wife and children, who are in hiding in Britain. Rebecca is helping them. Rachid wants him to kill a prominent Algerian in return for passports for himself and his family. Adam has a better offer: Malek forgets all about the assassination and gets free passports from MI5 for nothing.

Malek phones his wife to tell them he is coming to get them, but then overhears Free Islam terrorists killing Rebecca Sinclair and snatching his wife Samira, son Abdel and daughter Khalida.

Harry accuses Paul Seymour of concocting evidence. Juliet still wants Malek 'taken down' if the hit on the unknown Algerian target goes 'live'. The good news is that Malcolm has tracked down the mobile Rebecca Sinclair rang shortly before she was murdered. The owner is one Badrak Majdid. This leads the spooks to a very grim Kidbrooke housing estate. Majdid promises Malek his family's freedom if he carries out the hit. They will die if not. Not much of a choice. Especially when Malek gets to see seven-year-old son Abdel for the first time in two years.

The arrival in London of Algerian Bank President Abdelhak Rachmani reveals Malek's target. With Adam and Zaf on his tail, the ex-soldier drives to make the kill, unaware that Special Forces are on their way to storm the flat where Majdid is holding his family.

Fiona suggests they try the delicate approach – knock on the front door. That way Malek's family might get to stay alive. Zaf hunts for Malek, who has escaped to kill his target, with increasing desperation. As a Muslim, he objects to the way this man has been treated by the British state. Harry's direct order to kill Malek if he opens fire is ringing in his ears.

Posing as a rent officer, Fiona's front-door cunning gives Adam the chance to take the first guard out of play with a quick right hook. Special Forces go in. Cornered, Badrak Majdid takes Abdel hostage in the kitchen. Meanwhile, his father, marksman Malek, already has Rachmani lined up in his crosshairs.

Determined not to kill an innocent man, Zaf tries to convince Malek his family is safe, but Malek doesn't believe him. A sickened Zaf is about to open fire when Adam takes a last-ditch, desperate gamble, ordering Special Forces to fire through the shut door at Majdid, but keep the point of aim above the height of a small child. The gambit works – Majdid is shot dead.

As Malek is about to squeeze the trigger, Zaf lets him hear his son's voice. Harry is left to confront Paul Seymour. Very much less than amused, Juliet makes sure Seymour pays the price.

Malek and his family get a new life in Ireland. A happy ending all round. Even spooks have to win sometimes.

SPOOKS 4.7

DIRECTOR: OMAR MADHA

[Scriptwriter: Raymond Khoury]

' I'm just tired of continually living a lie. **Fiona Carter** '

In this episode, Fiona confronts the complex and murky past that is the lot of the experienced spy. A low-key, sombre flashback to a rainy London day six months before the present action. Fiona hides from Joumana, a Syrian woman she obviously once knew well. When she sees her, Joumana calls Fiona 'Amal'.

Back in the present, Syrian Foreign Minister Riyad Barzali flags that he wants to talk with MI5. Given that Syria is one of the world's most secretive and heavily policed states this is a rare and golden opportunity. It stars on George Bush's 'Axis of Evil' list. The only problem is Barzali's permanent shadow, his government minder Ali.

Fiona's reflection takes us into the back story: ten years before, her former husband and senior Syrian Intelligence heavy Farook captured an MI6 agent.

That agent was Adam. Adam had recruited Fiona to work for MI6 and they fell in love. Farook made Fiona watch as he beat Adam almost to death. In what seemed like the perfect revenge, Adam turned the tables. With Fiona's help he had Farook arrested and hanged – as a Mossad double-agent. Fiona, who still blames herself for Adam's ordeal, insists she wants to handle Barzali when he attends the opening of the new Syrian cultural centre.

FIONA This just came in from 6. It's from our ambassador in Damascus. He thinks he's found a possible way into the regime's inner circle.
HARRY And they say diplomacy doesn't work anymore.
FIONA Harry, I think this could be the breakthrough we've been waiting for. Nobody wants another Iraq least of all them, and if they're prepared to talk...

Dressed to the nines, Fiona flirts her way to Barzali. But she is in obvious danger and Adam is dead set against Fiona's involvement. Her go-anywhere PR cover, this time as 'Emma Stratstone', does nothing to stop Syrian embassy spook Basheer Shalhoob spotting and reporting her to the mukhabarat – Syrian secret police ['think KGB on steroids'].

Unaware she is already blown and in jeopardy, Fiona takes neophyte Jo – 'Vanessa' – along to the 'PR' meeting with Barzali. She also takes a gun with hollow-point bullets disguised as a remote control and a tiny personal GPS tracker taped to the back of her neck – both courtesy of Malcolm.

Jo has a gut feeling there is something dangerous below the surface here. Fiona lets Jo in on how she met, married and fell out with Farook, how he helped arrange a string of Tel Aviv suicide bombings, how Adam was trying to get to her husband through her and how they fell in love. Farook found out what was going on. He and his goons took revenge by beating and raping all Fiona/Amal's close female friends, including Joumana.

Over lunch, the MI5 waiter slips Barzali a drug in his mint sauce. Closely followed by the ever-watchful Ali, Barzali is rushed to hospital with suspected food poisoning. Here, Adam joins the action, in cover as Barzali's doctor. With Zaf and a colleague obliged to contrive an 'accident' to stop Syrian spooks following Fiona, the pressure builds.

Using fetching MI5 nurse Jenny to nudge Ali into buying a spiked coffee from the hospital vending machine, the spooks put him out of action long enough for Adam to snatch a few private words with Barzali. The Syrian Foreign Minister wants MI5 aid to effect regime change in Syria by helping to assassinate General Abu-Shawki, the feared head of the Syrian secret police. National Security Co-ordinator Juliet Shaw is for the plan; Harry is against it – but the most cogent opposition comes from Adam:

ADAM We could be doing the Syrian people a huge favour, but it could also plunge the country into a bloody mess. They don't deserve that. They've been through enough. And taking out an intelligence operative – that crosses the line. If they find out it was us, and they will find out, it'll be open season on our people. We'd be putting all our agents out there at risk.

At Juliet's suggestion, Adam asks Barzali to give MI5 the details of Iraqi insurgent operations across the Syrian border as a gesture of good faith. A step too far. When Barzali arrives back at his hotel, there's a surprise in store for him – and us. Farook isn't dead. He was never hanged. He's clutching a baseball bat, with which he now beats Barzali to death.

Going through the footage of the cultural centre reception Fiona, Ruth and Colin realise that Shalhoob recognised Fiona from the first. And Fiona knew it. She has to come off the op – Adam insists.

But Fiona is already ascending the stairs – alone – to the meeting with Barzali. Secretly, Fiona has been leading them all along. Haunted by the way Farook tortured Adam, she wants to confront her past and stop the Syrians ever hurting him again. She gets her wish: grabbing her over Barzali's dead body, Syrian goons take her to a car park and force her to change clothes. She loses her GPS tracker.

Waiting for her in the car outside is Farook – with a set of handcuffs. Her ex-husband has come to take 'lost lamb' Fiona back to Syria – where he intends 'having fun with her'. When Ruth discovers that Basheer Shalhoob is Farook's cousin, Adam finally understands. Beside himself, he attacks Shalhoob to make him reveal Fiona's whereabouts. But before he talks, the police arrive.

Colin's wizardry tracks Fiona to a remote airport where a chartered plane is waiting. Adam makes Harry ground all UK aircraft, buying him enough time to reach the field.

Locked in a Portakabin, Fiona slashes her arm with a piece of glass to feign suicide – and when Farook comes to her aid, stabs him in the neck with a long shard. She should have stabbed him harder – and more than once. As she runs towards Adam, Farook puts a bullet in Fiona's back. Leaving Adam without a wife and son Wes without a mother. Small consolation that Adam shoots Farook dead.

Fiona confronted her demons. But they proved too strong for her.

SPOOKS: BEHIND THE SCENES

SPOOKS 4.8

DIRECTOR: OMAR MADHA

[Scriptwriter: Howard Brenton]

'The dead past lies like a nightmare on the minds of the living. Karl Marx'

In another striking example of *Spooks* Syndrome – the ability to pre-figure soon-to-be-real events – we join Adam in a seedy London hotel, watching a news report about the funding crisis in the National Health Service. The action cuts to Her Majesty's Prison Buryhill. Wife Madeline welcomes seventy-three-year-old Soviet double-agent Hugo Ross on his release after thirty years inside. And Adam, bleeding on the inside, welcomes him with a spot of surveillance. It's so carelessly executed that Ross immediately spots him and chases him away.

Labour MP Robin Stackley enlists MI5's help. The government is selling London's bankrupt NHS hospitals off to Russian billionaire Oleg Korsakov. But 'Operation Songbird' – a contingency plan devised by Harry and Juliet to stop the deal means the Security Service is conspiring against an elected government. With the government convinced Korsakov is the Golden Goose that will save the NHS, and MI5 just as convinced he will asset-strip and destroy it, Harry comes down on the side of the greater good. Battle is joined.

Back in his 1975 timewarp home with Madeline, Hugo Ross drinks a toast to 'Comrade Boris Kandinsky', his former KGB handler.

Deep in post-traumatic stress, Adam can't confront the realities of Fiona's death. He has not even told their son that his mother is dead. Convinced – correctly – that Harry is giving him 'slops' when there is something big on, Adam demands more. Ordered to stay on Ross, Adam instead steals the Operation Songbird file.

Adam picked a good one: billionaire Korsakov has a mole inside GCHQ. Commercial analyst Sally Curtis is passing Korsakov secret intelligence via the lover Korsakov paid to seduce her.

The blanket anti-surveillance 'Faraday Cage' Korsakov has installed in his hotel suite prevents Zaf and the team from bugging him. With the NHS sell-off less than a week from triggering, Ruth suggests that Harry bring Adam back in from the cold. She meets frosty resistance. Harry thinks Adam needs psychiatric help – and it's hard to disagree.

Zaf, Jo and the team follow Sally Curtis and her 'stud' to a nightclub – with Adam in unofficial tow. But it's the much more experienced Adam who spots the coming 'hit' on Curtis. Her lover sticks her with an

injection of the chilling, British-developed, Cold War drug anaoxide diethylamide. The drug wipes Sally's memory, rendering her useless – and not just as an informant. She is now permanently brain-damaged.

Juliet Shaw has more bad news: Korsakov has been fast-tracked into British citizenship. Even worse, Stackley has a bad case of cold feet, stepping out of the conspiracy and insisting MI5 abandons Songbird, despite Juliet's taunting:

JULIET You asked us to start Songbird...
STACKLEY I was wrong. Korsakov has assured the Prime Minister of his moral standing. Now he's the only hope for the NHS. That's clear to me.
JULIET Is it? What have they offered you, you shabby little man?
STACKLEY Don't take that tone with me. I'm an elected representative. You two are just...servants. Stop the operation as you were told to do and leave Korsakov alone! Don't be reckless.
He walks away.
HARRY Breathtaking.
JULIET What're we gonna do?
HARRY Be reckless.

As ever, Harry has a cunning plan: use old communist Hugo (*left*) to entrap and disgrace 'new Russian' Korsakov. As a KGB double-agent, true communist Ross betrayed many British agents. More interesting still is Oleg Korsakov's real surname: Kandinsky. Oleg's KGB father ran double-agent Ross.

With the Faraday Cage still defying Malcolm's every attempt to bug his hotel suite, Korsakov gives Ross the Order of the Red Banner, the old Soviet Union's highest battlefield honour. He also offers the ex-con the job of writing the Kandinsky family history. Malcolm – having the worst day of his life' – is under intense pressure to defeat the Faraday Cage.

Back in his own cage, Adam is still swimming against the tide of his own grief – and threatening to go under.

With the deadline now less than twenty-four hours before the great sell-off, Harry tickles Ross. Korsakov made him an offer he could easily refuse: $100,000 to write the Kandinsky biography. But Harry makes Ross an offer he can't refuse:

HUGO Why don't you shoot him in the back of the neck? Oh sorry. The veneer of bourgeois democracy doesn't permit that.
HARRY What we need is information that will completely discredit him, something concrete, final. Hugo, I'm asking you to fight the good fight against capitalism, as you always have. I need you to bring down Korsakov.
HUGO (*laughing*) You are recruiting me to work for MI5?

As Korsakov puts Ross and Zaf through the torture of a seven-hour family history lesson, Ross starts to work Korsakov's boundless self-regard to MI5's advantage. Whenever Korsakov is about to damn himself out of his own mouth, he activates his protective anti-surveillance cage. But Malcolm finally manages to spike it. Suddenly, Ross exposes Zaf as a MI5 officer and offers to work as Korsakov's MI5 redoubled agent once Zaf has been 'disappeared'. Double-bluff, or betrayal?

Cool and purposeful under sentence of death, Zaf gets Korsakov to show his true face: 'What they think? My billions will save their pathetic socialistic Health Service? I will squeeze it for profit. Strip it bare. If hospital is on valuable land, sell it…let the market work.'

Adam calls in the troops. They are not quick enough to prevent Korsakov grabbing Ross and injecting him with a dose of the dreaded memory-wipe drug, but Adam has registered Sally Curtis's dreadful fate and brought an antidote. Adam's persistent, brilliant and unauthorised work has broken the case. Harry's praise finally opens the wellspring of Adam's grief.

Korsakov goes to a Russian prison. Adam is back on the team and – not least in telling his son Wes the truth – begins to deal with the fact of Fiona's death. And MI5 has stopped the government selling half the NHS down the river.

But the real sting lies in the tail: the anaoxide diethylamide antidote fails. Intellectual heavyweight Hugo Ross, looking forward to retirement, cannot remember the first lines of the *Communist Manifesto*. Or what it was he ever believed in. He has lost his mind.

```
MALCOLM'S BIG BAD HAIR DAY...
A 'Faraday Cage' is the reason lightning doesn't kill you
when it strikes a car. It is named after physicist Michael
Faraday. Gauss's law states that, since like electrical
charges repel each other, a like electrical charge will
migrate to the surface of any conducting object, and
therefore not penetrate it. Incredibly, Faraday built the
first such 'cage' in 1836. The application is useful, in
the case of our Russian billionaire friend, for blocking
all electromagnetically powered surveillance attempts.
```

SPOOKS 4.9

DIRECTOR: JULIAN SIMPSON

[Scriptwriter: Rupert Walters]

> **Just when did this country formally become a US colony?**
> **Harry Pearce**

With the USA rattling sabres at Iran, the CIA is rounding up the usual suspects – regardless of where in the world they happen to live. Courageously refusing to let the CIA 'render' – i.e. abduct – Iranian radical Lewis Khurvin, Harry puts his head on the official block. Not just with the CIA's London station chief Alex Roscoe, but, even more dangerously, with National Security Co-ordinator Juliet Shaw and No. 10.

Harry's stand against US extra-judicial abduction might have been right in principle, but when Khurvin apparently shoots dead two surveillance officers watching him, it looks as if Harry has made a terrible mistake.

JULIET Our relationship with the Americans is so important right now. No one wants a war with Iran ... You let the guy go, for God's sake.
HARRY It was a judgement call.
JULIET It was the wrong one!
HARRY So ... What?
JULIET If there was something I could do, I would.
HARRY looks at her, confused.
JULIET You're out Harry ... I'm sorry.

A bad beginning. Which gets worse when the spooks realise the double murder must mean Khurvin is on the point of executing a terrorist outrage in London. It's a view the CIA backs up by sending MI5 a photograph – which Malcolm verifies as genuine – purporting to show Khurvin training in Afghanistan.

By using the NSA's 'link analysis' software – as tweaked by Colin – the team is able to track Khurvin to Cardassia, a debt collection agency in Paternoster Square, London. Run by US citizen Nick Pollard, and equipped with a level of computer and office security suspiciously greater than its obvious needs, Adam targets Cardassia.

Tired of watching daytime TV quiz shows, Harry uses his friendly newsagent cut-out to contact Adam. Further foxing the MI5 surveillance breathing down his neck, Harry goes to the dogs – and meets Adam at the greyhound track to request the Khurvin dossier.

Working undercover as office cleaners, Adam and Jo sneak into Pollard's office. But Pollard – trained in counter-surveillance – does an about-face on the Millennium Bridge 'choke point'. Downloading the encrypted files from Pollard's computer – having first used an aerosol spray to detect and avoid his anti-surveillance laser beam – they exit with the data just in time. This guy is a professional. So what is he doing in a UK debt collection agency?

Ruth passes Harry the Khurvin file on the top deck of a bus– and their hands touch for a brief, scintillating moment. Given Pollard's training and hi-tech wizardry, Adam suspects he might be a CIA recruiting agent – and the whole Khurvin 'rendition' nothing more than a set-up – until Roscoe tells Juliet that Pollard is not with 'the Company'.

Harry loses his watchers. At the same time Ruth establishes through dental appointment records that Khurvin could not have been training in Afghanistan as per the photograph. The spooks are being played – but who is jerking the strings?

Ex-CIA agent Michael Gorman tells Harry that Pollard is a 'deniable', a clandestine agent in the UK to find and recruit disaffected Iranians, train them for terrorist action and get them to commit an atrocity so big and bad it will bounce the British and Americans into war with Iran. Pollard's masters are big oil and neo-con movers looking to profit from a fresh conflict. To help create the monster Khurvin has become, Pollard shot dead the two MI5 watchers.

Tailing Khurvin lights-off at night using night-vision goggles [like the BrixMis teams in the Cold War] leads them to the perimeter of London's Heathrow airport – where he picks up a cached Stinger Surface-to-Air Missile [SAM]. With less than ten seconds before the Iranian brings a large passenger jet crashing down onto the airport, Special Forces shoot him dead.

The team – with Harry back at the lead – pick Pollard up. And in a neat counter-reprise of the opening scene, we see Roscoe place fellow US citizen Pollard under arrest.

BRIXMIS

During the Cold War, covert British spying teams ran missions into Soviet Bloc states to collect mostly military intelligence. Usually in a specially tuned and extremely powerful car, the four-man teams included a specialist RCT [Royal Corps of Transport] driver, a so-called 'secret squirrel', a specialist comms expert from the Signallers and a couple of SAS/SBS troopers. One at least would have medical training, and one would be an expert photographer. The whole team had state-of-the-art knowledge of SovBloc military hardware. They also knew every variant of enemy uniform insignia – and had very good memories.

Operating mostly in East Germany – the glowing edge of the Cold War – BrixMis squads drove lights-off, at very high speeds, in darkness using NVGs to escape pursuit. Trained Russian and German linguists, members would often penetrate an enemy missile base or airfield, specify and count the weaponry and hope not to bump into a guard. Needless to say, many teams were involved in road traffic accidents – and quite a few people died trying to itemise the SovBloc order of battle. But BrixMis teams saw themselves as modern gladiators, stepping out into the arena to face down their Spetznatz and Vopo counterparts. In the deadly game of cat-and-mouse there were no rules – and dying was part of the risk.

SPOOKS 4.10

DIRECTOR: JULIAN SIMPSON
[Scriptwriter: Howard Brenton]

> **This is the *Coriolanus* nightmare. The greatest fighter in your army turns against you and everything you stand for. Harry Pearce**

Fired for 'being a drunk', ex-Royal Protection Squad officer Peter Haigh shoots himself dead while watching archive Princess Diana TV footage. A full year later, Haigh's ex-lover – and ex-MI5 super-spook – Angela Wells turns up in Ruth's living-room unannounced.

Angela – who believes the real reason Peter got fired is because he found out about the 'successful' Security Services plot to kill Di – wants to know why Haigh's stepsister, Ruth, didn't help him when she was at GCHQ. Ruth says there was nothing she could do. The idea that there was an official conspiracy to murder the Princess is insane.

But Angela takes a 'No Eyes' microfiche document out of the handy false tooth Malcolm made for her and lets Ruth read it on the microdot reader. Written by the 'Contingent Events Committee [CEC]', the file appears to show that Harry Pearce was the author of a joint MI5/MI6 assassination plot to kill 'P.D.' Angela wants Ruth to help her prove it.

Snooping in Harry's diary, Ruth sees that Harry was in fact in an unspecified meeting at 0900 hours on the day the CEC file was written. She begins to tell Adam. But she is overtaken by Angela Wells's arrival in person, 'smuggled in' by Juliet, who thinks she is just being nice to a former colleague. Juliet disappears to a Downing Street meeting as Malcolm comes and hugs his favourite, if delicately faded, Mata Hari.

But Angela has a little present for our spooks in her bag: a 'Concentrate 34' super-high-explosive bomb, remotely detonated by the triggering device she is holding. Ordering a Grid shut-down, Angela demands the team produce a chapter-and-verse account of how the security services assassinated the people's Princess. The 'proof' should be sent to all the major newspapers by dawn. If they do this, she will surrender. If not, the bomb will kill everyone and wreck Thames House.

Easy to miss in Angela's long list of demands is an update on the latest royal security protocols. Angela takes Jo into the meeting room. Jo tries to work on Angela, to 'personalise the situation'. Icy, professional and scary, Angela out-thinks Jo at every turn. While Jo attempts to subvert the enemy from within, Malcolm and Colin decide the bomb's triggering technology is too robust to mess with.

Adam makes a quick decision. He thinks Angela must have another agenda. But the best move is to 'prove' the conspiracy to her satisfaction. Harry claims the CEC never existed, and the whole idea of a conspiracy to assassinate Princess Diana is ridiculous. But given that they have to do something, Ruth gets the job of using the Grid's own database to help research the 'proof'.

Zaf – the first one to doubt Harry – lays out how a MI5/MI6 conspiracy might have actually worked. Oliver Mace – the vile Joint Intelligence Committee head – and equally obnoxious MI6 chief Jools Siviter arrive at Diana's hotel the day before her death. They arrange it so that Henri Paul – who is not drunk on duty – drives instead of the designated chauffeur, behind the wheel of a different, non-armoured Mercedes. Mace and Siviter also ensure that the blood samples supposedly taken from Paul post-mortem are switched for those of a very drunk suicide. They then have a motorbike pillion aim a 12-Hertz-per-second strobe light into Henri Paul's eyes in the Alma underpass, blinding him and killing Paul, Princess Diana and Dodi. 'At the 13th pillar. And Satan has his way'.

Ruth unearths quarantined Registry file tags. One of them is a CEC file tag. Adam and Ruth now confront Harry with the CEC tag and his diary entry. Harry owns up to planning Diana's death in Paris. 'The woman was unstable. There were fears she was being manipulated by undesirable influences. She was causing untold damage to the very central pillar of the British State, the Royal Family itself. It was felt if an accident could be arranged, there would be outpourings of grief which would paradoxically unite the nation.' And for a moment there, we all believe him – not least Ruth: 'You killed her.'

'What are you going to do?'

'Tell her[Angela]. And get Special Branch to arrest you for conspiracy to murder.'

Harry then breaks the fiction. The Contingent Events Committee was what it says on the tin. Contingency planning is brain-storming for worst-case scenarios. In one of these – the file Angela got hold of – the CEC thought through an attack on Diana's car by a motorbike pillion.

Reluctantly, Ruth first tells Angela the truth about the CEC and its 'worst-case scenario'. Then she tells Angela the big lie: that she – Ruth – and Peter once ran off to Blackpool for a 'mad week'. Peter was in love with her. 'Never with you.' A devastated Angela triggers the bomb.

But it doesn't explode. Ruth beats herself up about telling Angela lies in order to save everyone. But Harry is delighted with her. Colin discovers there was high explosive in Angela's bag – but no detonator. Harry and the team decide to treat Angela as 'a victim in the field' – provided she remains silent forever and leaves the country for good. Eerily penitent, she leaves.

Now the mechanism of the plot unwinds. Adam was right: Angela

Wells was toying with them, leading them by the nose. Predicting their every move, she has made off with a copy of the most recent report on new security measures at Buckingham Palace. Her real target is the Royal Family. Harry calls a 'Double A' alert – sending the Royal Family to 'Pegasus', its top-security bunker under St James's Palace.

Only trouble is, a check reveals Angela has spent seven months working there as an electrician. Once again, the spooks have played right into her hands. Down in the bunker, Malcolm detects explosives. The entire building is rigged to blow up, with the Royal Family in it.

When Malcolm freezes with fear, unable to cut the correct bomb wire, Adam steps in and cuts the lot. Gallantly, Adam tries to save Malcolm's pride – and reputation – by reporting him as the real hero. But Malcolm would rather own up.

There is one last twist: chewing the cud about the way Angela has played them for fools, Adam comes up with a novel way to 'help' Angela. Kill her.

Which is ironic. As the series ends, a blonde-haired sniper on the roofs above Thames House – who might or might not be Angela – takes aim and shoots Adam through the throat. Blood is pouring out of Adam's mouth. Surely he is either dead or dying. And Harry, the next target, is looking right down the barrel.

Is Adam leaving *Spooks* in the traditional manner? Will Harry suffer the same fate?

SPY SPEAK

JARGON-BUSTING...

One swallow does not make a summer. Well, okay – but what about a raven? The dark arts of deception have inspired a pretty vivid, if sometimes confusing, vocabulary, and both terms, in spook-speak, mean something completely different than birdlife.

Fiona, Adam's wife and an MI6 agent, is first introduced to us as a swallow – an agent who uses seduction as a means of control. In episode 3.4 she is brought into the MI5 fold when the team needs to entrap newspaper tycoon and rabid right-winger David Swift. Fiona escapes the chosen hotel with her dignity intact, but their target doesn't – the team frames Swift, mocking up images of Fiona as his beaten and raped victim. The millionaire's plot has been 'rolled up' and he is forced to leave the country.

Blink, and you might get lost in the murky depths of spook dialogue. In the very first episode, Harry, a veteran of the conflict in Northern Ireland, sets the scene with the enigmatic lines: 'Global terrorism, Islamic extremists, all phone tap resources plus ECHELON pointed at the Middle East, and now the old enemy looks like it's rearing its ugly head...'

Now, you might be able to work out who 'the old enemy' is – if you're British, that is – but what is 'ECHELON', and why is it 'pointed at the Middle East'? A scary group of listening super-computers run by the UK, USA and other English-speaking nations, ECHELON is the most powerful intelligence-gathering network in the world. Ever. But you could still be forgiven for missing or not understanding the reference. After all, it is still top secret.

Most importantly, in spook-speak, 'The Office' – as you might expect – is MI5 itself. 'The Friends' are MI6. Take a look at our quick guide and learn to talk the talk:

AN A–Z OF SPY TALK

Asset: a clandestine source or method, usually an agent.
Bagman: an agent who pays bribes to the authorities or is paymaster to a spy ring.
Bang and Burn: demolition and sabotage operations.
Birdwatcher: British slang for a spy.
Black Operations/Black Bag Job: covert deniable operations not attributable to the organisation performing them. Like trashing the computer databases of an institution deemed hostile – or inconvenient. Admit nothing, use a third party.
Blowback: a deception planted to mislead or destabilise another country that has bad unintended consequences – like arming the mujahideen in Afghanistan during the Russian occupation, giving rise to the Taliban.
Box: MI5. It's short for Box 500, one of the service's former postal addresses. Can also mean intelligence material.
Brush Pass: also known as a brush contact. A brief encounter where something is passed between a case officer and agent. The KGB favoured London's Brompton Oratory – lots of shady pews to choose from.
Camp Swampy: CIA's secret domestic training base (also known as 'The Farm').
Carnivore: an FBI system tapping an individual's email and Internet traffic. It is a specially designed 'Packet sniffer', or software program, that can log traffic on a digital network.
Center: KGB headquarters in Moscow.
Chicken Feed: convincing, but not critical, intelligence fed to mislead an enemy intelligence agency.
Chokepoint: a difficult area to cross without being seen, chosen to expose a tail. A bridge, a piazza – you get the idea.
Clearing the Coat-tails: getting your own spooks to make sure you are not being followed.
Cobbler: a spy who creates false passports, visas, diplomas and other documents.
COMINT: all intelligence gathered from intercepted communications.
The Company: an unofficial term for the CIA popularised by fiction.
Cover: the identity a spy assumes to achieve a mission.
Dead Drop: a secret location where materials can be left for another party to retrieve.
Dead Ground: an area not covered by surveillance, especially CCTV.
Discard: a service may allow some agents to be detected and arrested to protect other, more valuable 'assets'.
Dry Clean: checking to see if you are under surveillance. A favourite trick is diving into buildings and then coming out again.

ECHELON: a global communications listening network operated by English-language-speaking nations.

ELINT: electronic intelligence usually collected by technical interception.

Executive Action: assassination. The ultimate euphemism.

EXFIL: Exfiltration Operation: a rescue operation to bring a defector, refugee or operative out of a dangerous country or situation. As a young spook, current MI6 chief John Scarlett brought key Soviet defector Oleg Gordievsky out through Finland in the boot of his car.

Eyes Only: documents that may be read but not discussed and are burnt immediately after reading. Ears Only: too secret to even commit to writing.

The Firm: the Metropolitan Police's Special Branch – not to be confused with the Royal Family.

Friends: general slang for members of an allied intelligence service, and specifically British slang for members of the Secret Intelligence Service [MI6].

Ghoul: an officer who searches obituaries and graveyards for names of the dead that agents can adopt. See Frederick Forsyth's *The Day of the Jackal*.

Going Grey: blending in with the crowd, a basic surveillance technique. 14 Int & SY, the army's top secret undercover unit in Northern Ireland, used to make its male trainees practise looking at home anywhere, even in a lingerie shop.

Going Native: on an undercover operation it is not unknown for an agent to begin genuinely living their alias's life.

Honey Trap: slang for sexual use of men or women to intimidate or ensnare others.

HUMINT: intelligence collected by human sources, like agents.

Illegal: KGB/SVR operatives infiltrated into a target country without the protection of diplomatic immunity.

Illness: Russian slang for someone under arrest – at which point they are in 'hospital'.

INFIL: infiltration operation – planting an agent covertly, for example.

Invisibles: British nationals who are supporters of terrorist organisations.

Legend: a spy's claimed background or biography when operating undercover, supported by documents, details, bogus relatives, bank accounts and 'memories'.

Legoland: Terry Farrell's postmodern MI6 building at Vauxhall Cross. Also known as Babylon-on-Thames.

MASINT: measurement and signature intelligence. Uses elements that do not fit into the traditional scope of IMINT and SIGINT.

Mole: an agent of one organisation sent to penetrate a specific intelligence agency, usually by gaining employment.

Naked: a spy without cover or backup.

NSA: National Security Agency; or the 'No Such Agency'. US department dealing with breaking into the communications of other countries and protecting those of the USA.

Obbie: Police slang now adopted by the intelligence community for an observation – i.e. surveillance operation. Also obbie/obbo vans…

One-time Pad: sheets of paper/silk with strings of random numbers. Used as a one-off message key.

Open Source: intelligence gained from material that is already public.

ORBAT: an enemy agency's spying 'order of battle'. How many people they've got, and what they do.

Paroles: passwords to identify agents to each other.

PHOTINT: photographic intelligence, involving high-altitude reconnaissance using spy satellites or aircraft – or the people up the street in a van.

Pig: Russian intelligence term for a traitor.

Pocket Litter: items in a spy's pocket (receipts, coins, theatre tickets, etc.) that add authenticity to his or her identity.

Provocateur: someone who deliberately incites action to either entrap or politically embarrass [also agent provocateur].

Q Branch: the fictional part of the British intelligence service (MI6) that provides spy gadgetry to James Bond. 'A' Branch really provides what's known as 'Operational Support' – anything from CCTV coverage or covert entry specialists to surveillance units.

Rabbit: the target in a surveillance operation.

Raven: a male agent who seduces people for intelligence purposes.

Red: American name for an early Japanese Diplomatic cipher machine.

Retread: a retired officer reused as an agent or consultant. Hugo Ross, an ex-KGB double-agent in 4.8, becomes an MI5 agent.

Rezident [Resident]: KGB chief of a foreign station.

Rolled up: when an operation goes bad and an agent is arrested.

Sanitise: to delete specific material or revise documents.

Shoe: a false passport or visa.

SIGINT: signals intelligence, an amalgamation of COMINT and ELINT.

SITREP: a situation report, sent to CIA headquarters during an operation or crisis. A borrowing from the military.

SIS: Secret Intelligence Service, the official name for Britain's MI6. Also known as 'The Sister Service'.

Sleeper: an agent who acts only when a hostile situation develops – or to carry out a long pre-planned mission.

SMERSH: short for 'Smert Shpionam' (Death to Spies), the assassination division of the KGB.

Spook: MI5 slang for an operational officer.

Spy Dust: a chemical marking compound developed by the KGB to keep tabs on the activities of a target officer. Also called METKA. The compound is made of nitrophenyl pentadien (NPPD) and luminol.

Steganography: techniques for concealing the very existence of a message (secret inks or microdots).

Swallow: a female operative who may use sex as a trap or a tool. As Zoe in episode 3.6, or Mariela the Colombian drug baron's girlfriend in 2.9.

TECHINT: technical intelligence. Analysis of fielded equipment for training, research and the development of new weapons and equipment for eventual intelligence use.

Terminated: murdered. There are any number of other euphemisms for killing.

Timed Drop: a dead drop that will be retrieved by a recipient after a set time period.

Traffic Analysis: methods for gaining intelligence from the patterns and volumes of messages of radio intercepts.

Uncle: headquarters of any espionage service. Also means the mentor/controller in a close-target surveillance operation.

Walk-in: a defector who declares his or her intentions by walking into an official installation and asking for political asylum or volunteering to work in-place.

Watchers: surveillance professionals – MI5's 'A' Branch.

Wet Job: an operation where blood is shed.

Window Dressing: a cover story needs detail around it, to convince the opposition that it is real. The video rental store set up to entrap handsome bad man Rado into meeting and falling for Zoe is an example.

TOM What's George Smiley's favourite cocktail?
ZOE Moscow Mules...

BOYD You know how they call the real crazies
of my administration 'Vulcans'?
Harry nods.
BOYD Most of my boys have pointy ears...

TASH Oh yeah, what's the country ever done for me?
Harry sails into view.
HARRY ...Educated you. Provided you with
opportunities to find employment. Offered you
financial assistance if you can't. Looked after
you when you were sick. Ensured you were clothed,
housed and fed. Protected rather than persecuted
you and allowed you to choose your own government.
Actually you're one of the luckier citizens of
this planet.

ADAM I don't think the Americans or their
President have the appetite for another war.
HARRY When did that ever stop it from happening?

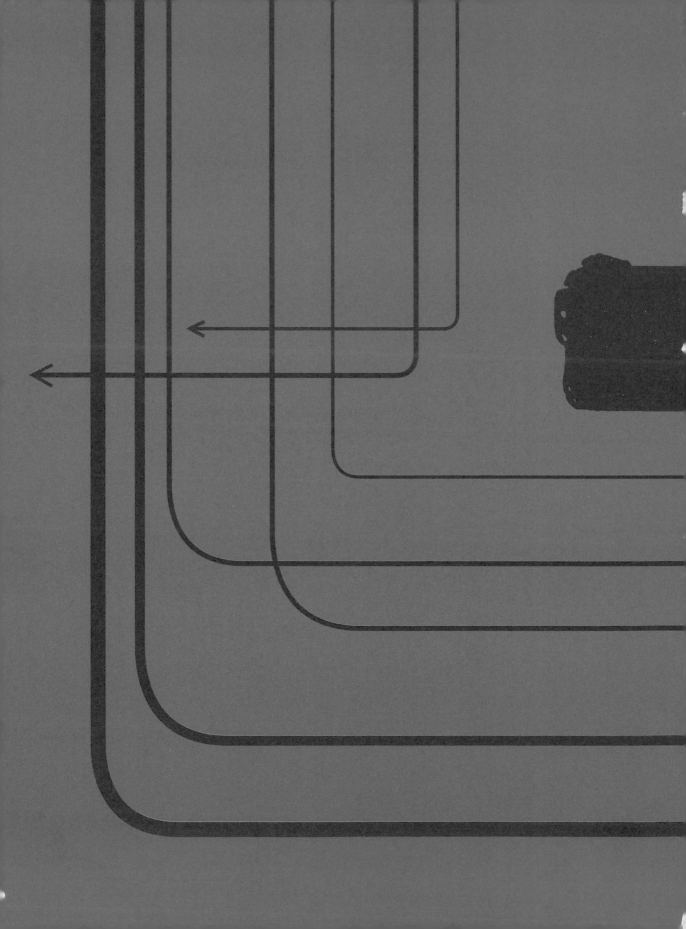